ELECTRICAL INTERFERENCE
AND PROTECTION

ELLIS HORWOOD SERIES IN ELECTRICAL AND ELECTRONIC ENGINEERING

Series Editor: PETER BRANDON,
Emeritus Professor of Electrical and Electronic Engineering, University of Cambridge

ELECTRONIC AND COMMUNICATION ENGINEERING

ELECTRICAL INTERFERENCE AND PROTECTION

E. THORNTON B.Sc.
Senior Principal Scientist, British Aerospace
Sowerby Research Centre, Bristol, and
formerly Senior Scientific Officer
Atomic Weapons Estabishment, Aldermaston

ELLIS HORWOOD
NEW YORK   LONDON   TORONTO   SYDNEY   TOKYO   SINGAPORE

First published in 1991 by
ELLIS HORWOOD LIMITED
Market Cross House, Cooper Street,
Chichester, West Sussex, PO19 1EB, England

A division of
Simon & Schuster International Group
A Paramount Communications Company

Typeset in Times by Ellis Horwood Limited
Printed and bound in Great Britain
by Bookcraft Ltd, Midsomer Norton, Avon

British Library Cataloguing-in-Publication Data

Thornton, E.
Electrical interference and protection. —
(Ellis Horwood series in electrical and electronic engineering)
I. Title. II. Series
621.382
ISBN 0–13–248238–X

Library of Congress Cataloging-in-Publication Data

Thornton, E. (Edward), 1933–
Electrical interference and protection / E. Thornton.
p. cm. — (Ellis Horwood series in electrical and electronic engineering. Electronic and
communication engineering)
Includes bibliographical references and index.
ISBN 0–13–248238–X
1. Electronic apparatus and appliances — Protection.
2. Electromagnetic interference. 3. Electromagnetic noise.
I. Title. II. Series.
TK7870.T46   1991
621.382'24–dc20

91–34623
CIP

Table of contents

*To Colyn Grey Morgan
who suggested writing this book
and my wife Helen
for her love and encouragement*

Preface

Electrical interference not only obscures desired signals but causes malfunctions which may be dangerous or disasterous. It is, by its nature, an unwanted, and therefore unpopular, form of electrical signal. As such, in the pulsed-power, telecommunications and wider electronics fields it is usually bitter experience and not precalculation that demonstrates the normality of interference signals. Perhaps this is due to a combination of the persistence of interference, human over-optimism, and a disinclination to quantify or even to accept the unwanted.

It is hoped to show that interference, like other physical phenomena, can be quantified using simple models, and by accepting it as normal, rather than the exception, to introduce it as an essential design concept. This has obvious time and cost advantages.

Electrical interference was previously most commonly met as a phenomenon in radio receivers but is now most associated with telecommunications, computers, and electronic control. The author's formal introduction was in the measurement of high transient currents associated with the discharge of high voltage capacitor banks. At the time, recording equipment was electronic-valve-operated; it has now been replaced by semiconductor-based recording systems a thousand times more sensitive.

In coming to grips with interference in a complex system the problem can appear formidable because of a wide range of possibilities for the injection and transfer of spurious signals. However, once it is remembered that they obey the same physical laws as the wanted signals, i.e. Maxwell's equations, they may be understood and then reduced. The author has found from working in the field of pulsed-power technology that most interference problems can be quantified by the use of simple models.

It is important to realize that the models are usually inexact and the results only approximate. This may be difficult for many scientists and engineers to accept until it is realized that the aim is to identify the source and its magnitude; high accuracy is not a prerequisite in order to reduce something. Using simple quantification to help select those modes of interference important in a particular case is an important tool in producing interference-free waveforms and in reducing spurious triggering.

The effect of lightning as a source of interference in telecommunications and electric power distribution has long been recognized. Nuclear-weapon electromagnetic pulse (EMP) has caused great concern in the military field and has resulted in extensive development and use of shielding techniques, together with establishment of specifications. Recent growth in the use of digital technology has brought the problems to industry and to comsumer electronics by increasing the opportunities for electromagnetic interaction. Shortly, EEC regulations will address the problem of electromagnetic emissions from all electrical devices and systems in Europe.

Full analytical solutions of interference injection into systems are usually extremely complex, and shielding techniques rely heavily on experiments and on simulation. The emphasis in this book is on basic physical processes rather than on complicated electromagnetic theory, and is on pulses rather than continuous-wave signals. This additional emphasis on wideband technology should interest physicists and digital engineers, and extend treatment beyond traditional radiofrequency (RF) engineering. Considering pulses ranging from those of millisecond duration to those of 100-ps risetime means that bandwidths from 100 Hz to 3 GHz at least must be considered.

Concentration on basic processes helps in understanding the overall electromagnetic similarity of a wide range of systems, ranging from large installations to the inside of an integrated circuit chip. Though interface is unwanted, its effective analysis and treatment is necessarily part of an in-depth study of the system involved, and therefore works towards the improvement of the latter.

ACKNOWLEDGEMENTS

Some responsibility for this monograph must be shared by C. Grey Morgan, and also by J. C. (Charlie) Martin, the former for suggesting its writing, and the latter indirectly for his guiding light in the spawning of so much pulsed power technology at AWE Aldermaston (and elsewhere), and in devising many diagnostic and shielding techniques. Acknowledgements are also due to members of his team, in particular to the late T. H. Storr.

Colleagues at AWE guided and assisted in much of the critical early pulsed power work, notably R. J. Wilson, P. T. G. Flynn, H. G. McPherson,

T. G. Taylor and R. S. Pitman. Additionally Electronic Engineering colleagues, mostly concerned with nuclear EMP (radio flash) were a most important source of radio-frequency electronic knowledge and techniques to one trained as a physicist. They included D. E. Lloyd, B. Elphick and R. Oats.

During cooperative work at AWE, W. L. Gagnon and P. Rupert, of Lawrence Livermore National Laboratory provided much useful and stimulating information on their extensive treatment of electrical interference problems in fusion lasers.

It is a pleasure to acknowledge the wealth of RF technical knowledge which H. D. Kitchin, of Bournlea Instruments made available, and his encouragement and hospitability during the early stages of writing.

At British Aerospace many colleagues have been responsible for making the author aware of the wider issues of electromagnetic compatibility, in particular, in BAe Dynamics, D. Morgan and his team, also D. McQuilton, T. R. Bowly, P. A. Holloway, and in BAe Military Aircraft, I. P. MacDiarmid and C. M. S. Jones. Also they have provided photographs for illustrations. J. Ackroyd, of Sowerby Research Centre has smoothed the administrative side when help was required in the later stages of publication.

Acknowledgements are due to Ray Proof Ltd, and to GEC Plessey Semiconductors Ltd, who have kindly provided photographs and drawings for illustration.

Finally the publishers, Ellis Horwood, and especially Sue Horwood, gave tactful encouragement and drive combined with patience over a number of years which were an essential ingredient, together with the strong support and encouragement of my wife Helen.

List of figures

Introduction

As complex semiconductor devices have become common in the domestic, industrial, and transport fields, electrical interference problems have become far more common than in the previously specialist areas such as telecommunications, nuclear EMP, and pulsed power. Malfunction and damage can be caused by mains transients and by directly radiated signals, in the latter case from the many types of fast-switching semiconductor devices. Although continuous-wave interference signals can interrupt communication systems it is usually in the high powers associated with transients that we look for energies sufficient to produce damage or serious malfunction in electronic systems or components. In the field of pulsed power, initially low electrical powers are converted into high power transients, and it is similar physical mechanisms which frequently result in the generation of unwanted transients.

It is in this field also that the highest power manmade electrical pulses are generated and measured, in excess of 10^{13} W. This exceeds the continuous electrical generating capacity of any country, and equals the power, but not the energy, in a typical lightning flash.

To safely operate and monitor such high power pulse generators requires careful and extensive use of shielding techniques. For this reason the author considers it an ideal field from which to approach the problem of electrical interference.

Electrical interference has long been recognized in radio communications, and many of the principles and techniques of shielding were established in the first half of this century. The advent of high power RF pulses in radar in the Second World War gave impetus to the problem, but it is the EMP from nuclear detonations which has produced the greatest awareness of interference. Concern about the effects on a wide range of military and strategic civil electronic systems has led to extensive studies and measurements, and the establishment of a discipline of electromagnetic compatibility (Morgan, 1983). Extensive shielding techniques have been much developed and a wide range of specialized hardware has become available, for example, shielded rooms, conducting gaskets and coaxial cables with solid outer conductor. Proliferation of consumer electronic equipment has extended the problem far beyond the military field, though at present it is still in the fields of nuclear effects simulation and nuclear fusion that the highest-power pulse generators are to be found, and therefore where the most interesting diagnostics shielding problems are likely to be found.

RF technologists may work with received signals of a few microvolts, i.e. with powers of 10^{-13} W, and with maximum generated powers of 1 MW. However, such low received powers would normally be in the remote far field of the transmitter where the inverse square law of transmission introduces a large additional attenuation factor, Shielding attenuation factors of 10^{10} (100 dB) are usually adequate, which is typically that of a commercial screened room. In contrast a pulsed-power technologist may be monitoring a diagnostic signal of 10 mV, or 1 μW into 100 Ω impedance, close to a generator of 10^{12} W. In these near-field conditions a shielding attenuation factor of 10^{18} (180 dB) is required. If a shielded room of 100 dB is used, the additional 80 dB of attenuation must be obtained by careful circuit configuration and additional shielding.

Two important themes of this book are so obvious that it must demonstrate the enormous power of human optimism that they are so frequently forgotten or ignored, at least in the laboratory.

Firstly:

Electrical interference will always occur; it is the norm.

Secondly:

Electrical interference is usually most easily and cost-effectively removed at, or close to, its source.

It follows logically that shielding of a pulsed-power source or other interference generator should be an automatic design procedure.

That this approach works was demonstrated to the author during commissioning of the pulsed relativistic electron beam machine EROS at AWE Aldermaston, a device of about 10^{12} W electrical power. It proved possible to completely enclose the 200-ton machine in an effectively continuous metal shield, to decouple all metallic connections to it, and even to interpose a thin layer of insulation between its base and the floor. At the time (1968) initial diagnostic measurements were made using high-bandwidth, vacuum-valve oscilloscopes of sensitivity 30 V/div standing close alongside the machine.

Interference signal levels less than 10 V were obtained, an attenuation level of 120 dB less than the main pulse. Previously, unenclosed pulsed machines of two and three orders of magnitude less power had produced larger levels of interference. When transistor oscilloscopes in a shielded room were later added to the EROS facility, signals of 10 mW amplitude could be monitored.

On the ETA2 machine at Lawrence Livermore National Laboratory, California, the interference level on the electron beam current monitor was so low (1989) that it was possible to record clean waveforms of isolated parts of the electron beam carrying only 0.1% of the main current.

It is on large installations like these that the importance of electrical shielding as a design concept is most likely to be appreciated, owing to the difficulties of making modifications at a later stage.

Nuclear EMP, its effects and shielding have been extensively studied for over 30 years. Though considerable unclassified literature is now available, treatments are usually mathematically complex and are naturally biased towards the military field. Nuclear EMP effects are usually in the far field of the source, where the electromagnetic field can easily be determined. The effects on simple shapes can be determined, but it is in complex structures that the mathematics may be too difficult, and the use of simpler models or laboratory simulation may be the only solution. Increasing use of digital and computer control in the commercial field has created many more interference problems, for instance in fly-by-wire airliners. Nuclear EMP technology is probably a good starting point for studying many of them.

Aircraft, electrical power lines and telecommunications are susceptible to lightning, which deserves separate mention. Though the currents which flow in lightning strokes can be simulated for microsecond times in the laboratory, the strokes are of millisecond duration, and large charges flow, producing additional effects. Generally large pulsed-power facilities are required to simulate these pulses, such as the Lightning Test and Technology Unit at Culham Laboratory.

The author's approach is generally based on single-shot high power pulse technology, which is laboratory-based. This has three distinct advantages:

(1) Interference source and receiver are close together, and near-field conditions apply. This promotes a full systems approach and examination of all possible coupling mechanisms.

(2) Single fast-risetime pulses have a wide fequency spectrum, requiring a broadband approach. Outside the telecommunications field transients are the most likely source of interference, and even within it digital technology is becoming common.

(3) The high peak currents involved (above 10^3 A) develop high inductive electromotive forces (EMFs) in even massive conductors, giving rise to

the important concept of ground (earth) loops. Though less apparent, this important concept is still crucial in controlling interference even in small, low power semiconductor systems. High pulse power currents and high voltages also introduce non-linear effects, such as sparking, which can produce further interference at frequencies remote from that of the primary source. They are concepts and effects of concern outside pulsed-power laboratories and the military.

The large ground-loop EMFs produced in pulsed-power systems have their analogy in the loop signals at low frequencies resulting from rectification and smoothing in low voltage power supplies (in our concepts low means less than mains potential). In multiple-grounded circuits in audio and hi-fi systems they can appear as hum, and may cause interference in equipment measuring very small DC or low frequency signals. Likewise the thin tracks of printed circuit boards and the thinner still tracks within integrated circuit chips are analogous ground loops, the effects of which may be crucial.

In practice it is usually the identification and control of individual circuit looops and other coupling elements which present the main problems, once the basic physical mechanisms of interference have been mastered. The mechanisms which result in interference generation and transfer are relatively simple. Lack of understanding of them means that interference problems can be solved by reference to documentation and specifications only in limited cases.

The ground loops in large capacitor-bank installations can be very complex. They may not only comprise the main discharge leads and diagnostic cables, but also involve the whole of the mains wiring of the surrounding building structure. Through metallic contact, or simply through stray capacitances at high frequencies, the building services (e.g. water and gases) in metal pipes, the building structure, if metallic, and reinforcing bars in concrete may become involved in the transfer of electromagnetic energy.

Overall control of these factors is necessary for successful reduction of interference, and in the limit all metallic objects should be considered and their effects quantified if possible. Even for non-quantifiable effects a conscious decision should be taken, even if it includes the extremes of doing nothing or of grossly overshielding. The theoretical ideal solution, that of providing a complete Faraday shield, is not always practicable.

It is hoped to demonstrate that the interference level, though it may be difficult to quantify accurately, is nevertheless built into systems during their design and construction. As installations may be large, complex, and closely integrated into their laboratory or building, it follows that later reduction of interference levels may prove very difficult. So it is strongly emphasized that interference merits treatment as a total systems concept from the outset.

Making necessary alterations in scale to microscopic size, the same comments apply to large-scale integration semiconductor systems and indeed to those of intermediate size. That similar comments apply over such a wide dimensional range should not be surprising, for the governing physical laws are the same. Large, multiple-module installations, such as those storing high energies in fusion research lasers, or those working at high average powers by rapid repetition in industrial lasers, merit particular attention to interference problems. This is especially so with the increasing use of sensitive semiconductor control and diagnostic circuitry. Use of software control, with the attendant possibility of expensive or dangerous malfunction adds further emphasis.

Avoidance of ground loops is a well-established principle in pulsed power as well as in hi-fi, and in the former can result in personnel hazards as well as interference during operation. For this reason electrical safety should be considered as part of interference treatment. Implementation of electrical safety requirements under pulse conditions may appear to involve opposing principles, namely provision of extensive grounding while simultaneously avoiding ground loops.

We hope to establish the basic ways in which interference is generated in simplified, but representative, circuits and systems and to estimate the signal levels. We shall then consider the modification of signals by more complex circuitry and by changes in the frequency components. Different sources of interference are considered, and practical means of reduction both at source and in diagnostics are discussed in detail.

As a last point, introduction of the 1992 EEC regulations on electromagnetic emissions should have wide-ranging implications in this field because they cover emission from all electrical equipment.

REFERENCE

Morgan, D. (1983), *An introduction to electromagnetic compatibility*, IEE Summer School Lectures, University of Canterbury, 1983.

1

Basic concepts

1.1 DEFINITIONS AND SUBJECT TREATMENT

Electrical interference is, by definition, an unwanted signal, but so is electrical noise, from which, for the purpose of this treatment, it will be distinguished.

Herein, noise is considered a signal generated spontaneously and randomly within the elements of a circuit owing to the fundamental physical properties of those elements and usually associated with statistical electronic processes such as shot and Johnson noise.

Interference is considered as a signal within the elements of a circuit which has been produced by coupling from another signal external to the circuit or from elsewhere in the circuit.

The energy to generate noise comes, therefore, from within the elements themselves, while that in interference is transferred by electromagnetic coupling from elsewhere. There may be limiting cases, particularly at low signal levels, where there is not a sharply defined distinction between the two, but in most practical cases of the kind which we will consider, the definition is adequate.

Noise in electronic devices is cause by random movements of electrons under thermal agitation (Johnson noise), and by statistical fluctuations in electric currents due to their discreet electron nature (shot noise), the latter being modified in semiconductors by various types of potential barriers (Bell, 1960; Buckingham, 1983). Some understanding of the physics of these processes is useful in the study of interference and in particular the fundamental noise levels determine where further interference reduction is impossible. An inherently noisy network can be considered as a noise-free network connected to a noise generator. To this extent it is similar to an interference generator in that there is a signal transfer.

An additional similarity should be carefully considered. The noise signal in a network may be altered by modifying the network. This will not only change the network response, but also alter the noise source. Since interference is produced by coupling energy into a circuit, modification of the circuit elements to attenuate the signal in it may also alter the coupling to the source. We consider interference as a process of electromagnetic energy transfer from a source to a receiver, through the intermediate stage of a coupling mechanism, thence to a circuit network, which is itself connected to the receiver (see Fig. 1.1).

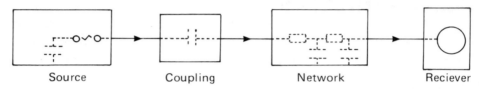

Source   Coupling   Network   Reciever

Fig. 1.1 — Electromagnetic energy transfer sequence.

This basic sequence is important and should be kept in mind for the following reasons:

(1) The problem can be broken down into sequential parts for treatment, and it is obvious that the interface signal may, in principle, be reduced in one or more of these parts.

(2) The different parts may interact with each other, so that alteration of one part to attenuate the signal it sends out may actually increase the signal it receives. It is this crucial fact, which is so frequently ignored, that eventually compels one to take interference seriously as a total systems concept. Close interaction of all the components in the sequence is a feature of most pulsed-power systems in comparison with many RF systems where the receiver is in the remote far field of the source.

(3) Thirdly, but not least important, the sequence clearly illustrates the recurring theme that interference is best reduced at source. Quite often the other methods of 'reduction' cause an increase when first tried out; source reduction is guaranteed!

Treatment of interference usually starts with identification of the source, followed by a consideration of the coupling mechanisms to the receiver through the associated circuit. Estimation of the magnitudes of the induced and transmitted signals and comparison with observed magnitudes, where possible, will ideally identify the interference path. Then the means of reduction can be investigated by changing component values, by decoupling, or by the use of available shielding hardware. This is the ideal, for in practice the interference path is not always obvoius, and some degree of trial and error is inevitable. When this sequential approach is not possible, for instance when the interface source is inaccessible, the only possible treatment may be shielding of the receiver, and this may be both expensive and bulky.

To summarize, so far we have stated that interference has a source and a coupling mechanism into a circuit system which itself couples into a receiver. The parts may themselves be multiple and complex, and understanding and control of individual parts is the basis of successful reduction. At the outset the problem may be approached in two ways, depending on whether the interference engineer has or has not control of the interference source. As reduction at source is the most effective, it is a high priority for the interference engineer to establish a maximum of control over the system or project. This can be very difficult if other project engineers or scientists are unaware of the adverse consequences of interference!

Interference may occur in continuous or in transient form: at the one extreme it may momentarily distort speech in a communications system, and at the other it may interfere with the control system in a large installation such as an aircraft or a power station, causing an expensive or disastrous malfunction. Perhaps intermediate between these extremes lies the technology of recording and displaying the diagnostic signals of repetitive, and in particular single-shot, phenomena. Where signals are being displayed and the interference signal shows up alongside the desired signal, both can be recorded for study. With this initial approach time resolution has been introduced as a useful diagnostic technique.

Interruptions and fluctuations in the mains supply can cause interference, though they are usually outside user control. In critical systems, e.g. computers, protection can be provided by backup batteries, including, if necessary, mains inverters. Fluctuations may result in the production of fast transients in the main wiring, for instance through the tripping of circuit breakers. These and other fast transients in the mains will be considered in a later chapter. Consideration of mains transients is a reminder of the vulnerability of computers and digital systems generally to interference in a way does not normally affect analogue systems. Excluding permanent damage to components, an analogue system is only corrupted during and shortly after the interference pulse. A digital system can be corrupted in the same way, but in addition may have its memory storage permanently corrupted. Our definition of interference is an undesired signal, and an undesired signal is one which prevents proper operation of the electrical system in question.

We shall start by considering the interference problems encountered in the generation of high power pulses, typically kilovolts and kiloamps. As these can occur in timescales from less than 1 ns, to over 1 ms, they present shielding problems from microwave to audio frequencies. This seems a good standpoint for treatment, since the analysis and techniques to be discussed should be widely applicable after making due allowance for frequency-dependent effects. The high powers can be scaled upwards, or down to the very low powers of digital circuitry, often simply by application of Ohm's law, or more strictly by applying Maxwell's equations. There is one notable exception to this scaling, and that is when the high voltages and currents induce non-linear effects such as sparking and flashover.

1.2   GENERATION OF THE INTERFERENCE PULSE

It is fundamentally important to determine where and how the interference signal is generated, for it determines in turn the physical mechanisms and magnitudes involved in energy transfer.

It may originate from outside or inside the system. Within the system it may result from a fault, or from a correct operating signal, some energy from which is transferred by a coupling mechanism into part of the system in which it is not desired. The usual RF view of interference is that of an antenna, perhaps a dipole, radiating the undesired signal to the remote far field. At this point it can be characterized as a plane electromagnetic wave of known field strength, measured in volts per metre. Here also it is picked up by induction in antenna-like wires, or loops or on a surface, from which it is transferred to the receiver. In contrast the pulsed-power concept is that of a source of a high voltage, high current transient, directly coupled in the close near field by a number of mechanisms to the associated circuit and receiver. The mechanisms which we will consider are as follows:

(1) Mutual inductance between the conductor carrying the primary current and a nearby circuit loop.
(2) Stray capacitance from a primary conductor carrying a high voltage transient to a nearby circuit conductor.
(3) A large EMF existing along the length of a primary conductor by virtue of the high current flowing through it and its finite inductance and resistance. If there are a number of external connections to this conductor the EMF can drive current into the external circutis.

These mechanisms both transfer interference signals in a system and convert correct signals in one part into interference elsewhere. Mechanism

(3) is a most common form interference generator in pulsed power but is less well known in other fields where much smaller currents are involved. It is, however, well-known in hi-fi as a means by which mains hum is injected into sensitive audio amplifiers. More recently it has become known in printed circuits and integrated circuits, where the circuit conductors can be very thin and narrow. This ground, or earth-loop current is very important and will be given considerable attention in the next chapter. Experience has shown that it is an effect frequently ignored in practice, though EMFs of kilovolts can easily be generated along short lengths of even the most massive conductors. The inductance of the conductor is primarily determined by its length and not by its cross-section and its resistance is enhanced considerably by the skin effect. The existence of more then one external connection to this nominally zero potential lead can drive considerable currents round external loops, giving a range of secondary interference effects.

Coaxial cables are frequently used for monitoring and trigger leads, and their braids create an additional source of interference for consideration. As is fairly well known in the field of RF technology, a current flowing along the braid of a coaxial cable such as a ground-loop current, will inject a signal into the cable. This is because the woven braid is an imperfect shield (Oats, 1971; Lee, 1986).

The mechanisms of generation proposed above, involving inductance, capacitance and the skin effect, are frequency-dependent, Some effects increase and other decrease as the frequency increases, and this is important in establishing which is the principal mechanism in a particular case. In fact it can sometimes simplify an otherwise daunting problem. At very high frequencies the finite velocity of light can have a profound effect on the generation and propagation of interference signals, for the signal arrives at different parts of the circuit at different times. A change from lumped to distributed circuit parameters becomes necessary in the treatment.

As suggested already, an interference signal is not always completely foreign to the system; it may have the same waveshape as the main discharge, or as the diagnostic signal, and when, as interference, it is superimposed on the desired signal, it may be particularly difficult to separate from it. If only the waveshape is required, this in unimportant, but if the magnitude is required it could be critical. However, most interference is of a different waveshape from the desired signal. Triggered spark gaps are frequently used as high current switches, and the fast triggering transient is to be seen at the beginning of many recorded waveforms. Its voltage amplitude can exceed the switch voltage, and its interference amplitude can likewise exceed that of the diagnostic signal. It can be quite a challenge to reduce it significantly, though in some instances it may not seriously obscure the slower main signal. In fact in some instances it may be used as a fiducial reference marker, or even used to trigger the oscilloscope, often unintentionally! Switch transients can be a very serious problem in complex systems, causing, among other faults, premature triggering of other stages.

1.3 THEORETICAL TECHNIQUES

Some background and introduction to interference generation has been given in the previous two sections, and here the process is extended to estimate transferred signal levels, usually by the determination of relevant circuit impedances. The simplified solutions of Maxwell's equations used are essentially forms of Ohm's law, taking into account circuit reactances in addition to, or instead of, resistances. Near-field conditions are assumed except in specific cases when appreciable transient-time effects are present. The latter are usually considered as transmission line problems associated with a characteristics impedance and propagation time.

To those already versed in electromagnetic theory the equations used are simple and basic, and the ranges of frequency are likley to be familiar to most readers. However, the voltage and current magnitudes met, and the fact that they are mostly due to invisible circuit strays rather than to visible components, are probably unfamiliar. It is the visualization of these strays, and the recognition that they, and Maxwell's equations, are fully three-dimensional in effect and concept that is most vital.

Circuit impedances can usually be calculated from purely geometrical considerations using standard formulae, e.g. Lewis and Wells (1956). Millman and Taub (1965), Knoepfel (1970), Adler (1989). A number of frequently used formulae are collected together in this section. Examination of the formulae shows that a number of them are of logarithmic or inverse ratio of dimensions. This means that over the relatively wide range of dimensions met in practice, the corresponding range of impedances is small. It justifies the simple treatment by enabling adequate accuracy to be obtained from impedances estimated only roughly by visual inspection.

The inductance, capacitance, and impedance of common conductor geometries are given in Table 1.1 and derived numerical examples are shown in Table 1.2. The figures refer to air (vacuum) dielectric, and capacitances with other dielectrics should be multiplied by ε and impedance divided by $\varepsilon^{1/2}$.

To complete this chapter we will briefly consider the skin effect on conductors and the transfer impedance in coaxial lines, since both are important in quantifying interference levels.

The skin depth in a conductor is given, e.g. Lewis and Wells, 1956; Adler, 1989) by:

Table 1.1 — Inductance, capacitance and impedance of common conductor geometries

Configuration	Inductance	Capacitance	Impedance
Parallel strips $b \gg a$	$4\pi \times 10^{-7}(a/b)$ H/m	$8.85 \times 10^{-12}(b/a)$ F/m	$377a/b\ \Omega$
Coaxial cylinders	$2 \times 10^{-7}\log_e(b/a)$ H/m	$\dfrac{5.56 \times 10^{-11}}{\log_e(b/a)}$ F/m	$60\log_e(b/a)\ \Omega$
Flat discs $t \ll a$	$2t\log_e(b/a) \times 10^{-7}$ H	$2.78 \times 10^{-11}(b^2 - a^2)/t$ F	$60\,t/r\ \Omega$ (at r)
Parallel equal cylinders	$4 \times 10^{-7}\log_e(D/r)$ H/m	$\dfrac{2.78 \times 10^{-11}}{\log_e(D/r)}$ F/m	$120\log_e(D/r)\ \Omega$
Parallel cylinder and plane	$2 \times 10^{-7}\log_e(2D/r)$ H/m	$\dfrac{5.56 \times 10^{-11}}{\log_e[2D - r)/r]}$ F/m	$60\log_e(2D/r)\ \Omega$
Concentric spheres		$110 \times 10^{-12}ab/(b - a)$ F	
Isolated sphere		$110 \times 10^{-12}r$ F	

Table 1.2 — Numerical values of inductance, capacitance and impedance

Configuration		Inductance	Capacitance	Impedance
Parallel strips	100×1 mm	12.6 nH/m	0.89 nF/m	3.8 Ω
	100×13 mm	166 nH/m	68 pF/m	50 Ω
Coaxial cylinders	$b = 100$ mm, $a = 95$ mm	10.3 nH/m	1.1 nF/m	3.1 Ω
	100 mm 1 mm	0.92 μH/m	12 pF/m	276 Ω
Parallel wires	$r = 1$ mm, $D = 10$ mm	0.92 μH/m	12 pF/m	276 Ω
Wire and plane	$r = 1$ mm, $D = 10$ mm	0.6 μH/m	19 pF/m	180 Ω
Concentric spheres	$b = 100$ mm, $a = 95$ mm		0.2 nF	
	100 mm, 10 mm		1.2 pF	
Isolated sphere	$r = 100$ mm		11 pF	

$$\delta = (\rho/\pi\mu f)^{1/2}$$

$$\simeq 5.1 \times 10^2 (\rho/f)^{1/2} \text{ m for non-magnetic metals.}$$

In copper ($\rho = 1.7 \times 10^{-8} \, \Omega\text{m}$), $\delta \simeq 20 \, \mu\text{m}$ at 10 MHz, so that conductor resistances at high frequency will normally greatly exceed the DC resistance.

The transfer impedance Z_τ of a coaxial line (e.g. Oats 1971, Lee 1986) is defined as the injected signal per unit length of line resulting from unit current flowing in the braid.

In a typical single-braided coax $Z_\tau \simeq 10 \, \text{m}\Omega/\text{m}$, up to 100 kHz, increasing to 100 mΩ/m at 10 MHz. In a double-screened coaxial line the transfer impedance is similar at low frequencies, but falls to around 1 mΩ/m at 10 MHz. In semi-rigid (solid-shield) cables Z_τ falls rapidly above 100 kHz, and is less than 0.1 mΩ/m at 10 MHz.

REFERENCES

Adler, R. J. (1989) *Pulsed Power Formulary*. North Star Research Corporation.

Bell, D. A. (1960) *Electrical noise*. Van Nostrand.

Buckingham, M. J. (1983) *Noise in electromagnetic devices and systems*. Ellis Horwood.

Knoepfel, H. (1970) *Pulsed high magnetic fields*, North Holland.

Lee, K. H. S. (1986) *EMP interaction: principles, techniques and reference data*. Hemisphere.

Lewis, I. A. D. & Wells, F. H. (1956) *Millimicrosecond pulse techniques*. Pergamon Press.

Millman, J. & Taub, H. (1965) *Pulse, digital and switching waveforms*. McGraw-Hill.

Oats, R. (1971) *Reponse of electrically short cables to transient electromagnetic fields*. AWRE Report No. 47/71., HMSO.

2

Sources of interference and the ground loop

2.1 FEATURES OF INTERFERENCE SOURCES

Early recognition of interference in radio communications has probably resulted in its general conception as a phenomenon generated in the remote far field relative to the receiver. The effects of lightning on power and telephone lines, and, more recently, the effects of nuclear EMP have also tended to be treated as remote-source phenomena. The growth of pulsed-power technology, and the close-up diagnostics of nuclear weapons, for example in underground tests, place more emphasis on treatment as a near-field phenomenon. At the time of writing, there is a considerable growth in the industrial and domestic use of digital devices, and therefore a corresponding concern with interference generated in precisely those environments. Again the likely emphasis seems towards near-field phenomena.

Before attempting to quantify the transmitted interference singals it is vital to give some consideration as to the nature of the source. In the previous chapter we pointed out that low level signals merge into those due to inherent thermal and statistical fluctuation processes in the particular system. These latter are likely to be at levels below 1 mV in a typical electronic system. Signals of this level are common in operational amplifiers, but in purely digital circuitry levels of about 1 V are required to interfere with normal working, that is a factor of 10^3 in voltage or 10^6 in power higher than inherent (non-fault) noise. The most likely source of signals above the 1V level are high power systems and transients.

Transient signals, being rich in high frequency components, usually couple more easily into intermediate circuits. Semiconductors are also susceptible to damage at levels only an order of magnitude higher than those which just cause misoperation. This is because their junctions usually have low voltage breakdown and low thermal capacity. We can start analysing possible transient sources by classifying them as follows:

(1) Pulsed-power transients intentionally generated by the operator.
(2) Pulsed power transients directly, but randomly, generated outside the operator's immediate control, e.g. lightning, or a misfire.
(3) Transients generated indirectly, by an interruption in a non-pulsed electrical system, e.g. power supply, or by a spark or high voltage flashover.

In the third category are signals of considerably higher power than the DC power of the undisturbed system. What we hope to demonstrate, if it is not already becoming apparent from the above classification is that in their basic physical nature the categories are essentially similar. This means that, in the first category, the source can be considered as a controlled pulse generator. Obviously, transients in the second category are similar in many electrical characteristics to the first, as also are the third.

High power pulses can be generated in a number of ways, which can usually be broken down into variants of three basic sources. These are the discharge of a charged capacitor, the discharge of a charged transmission line, and the interruption of the steady current flowing through an inductance. Of these the first is the most common and will be considered in some detail.

2.2 CAPACITOR DISCHARGE CIRCUIT

Fig. 2.1 is a schematic of this common circuit, where capacitor C is initially charged to voltage V_0. At time $t = 0$ switch S is closed and the capacitor discharges into load inductance L and resistance R. When $R < (4L/C)^{1/2}$ (underdamped) the classical damped sinusoid waveform for current I is given (e.g. Starling, 1941; Millman and Taub, 1965; or Halliday and Resnick, 1966) by:

$$I = V_0 \left(\frac{C}{L}\right)^{1/2} \exp\left(-\frac{Rt}{2L}\right) \sin\left(\frac{I}{LC} - \left(\frac{R}{2L}\right)^2\right)^{1/2} t \qquad (2.1)$$

$$I_{max} = V_0(C/L)^{1/2} \qquad (2.2)$$

In the critically damped case, $R = (4L/C)^{1/2}$, and:

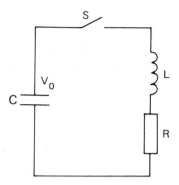

Fig. 2.1 — CLR circuit.

$$I = \frac{V_0 t}{L} \exp\left(\frac{-Rt}{2L}\right) \tag{2.3}$$

$$I_{max} = \frac{V_0}{e}\left(\frac{C}{L}\right)^{1/2} \tag{2.4}$$

In order to consider how the circuit of Fig. 2.1 can generate interference, let us assume some component values which might exist in a small capacitor bank in which some effort has been made to ensure a large peak current by keeping the inductance relatively low (eq. 2.1):

$$C = 10\,\mu F, \quad L = 100\,nH, \quad V_0 = 20\,kV \ .$$

Fig. 2.2 shows waveforms for zero and critical damping. We note that the peak current in Fig. 2.2 is 200 kA and the time to first peak current 1.5 μs. It is now time to ask how this circuit can generate interference, and to start answering we first replace Fig. 2.2 by a configuration closer to real practice, such as Fig. 2.3.

In Fig. 2.3 the main circuit parameters are unchanged, but the switch has been replaced by a triggered spark gap, with midplane electrode, so that the main discharge can be precisely switched in the time domain. Power supply, control, and trigger unit, together with a diagnostic voltage probe, have been added. Note particularly that these units have separate ground leads, mostly through their mains leads. Also it is critically important to note that the circuit inductance of 100 nH has been separated into four separate components. This is a fairly low inductance, and is that of a narrow loop of two parallel conductors 10 cm wide, and approximately 1 m long, separated by only 1 cm, using the inductance formula in the previous chapter. The loop

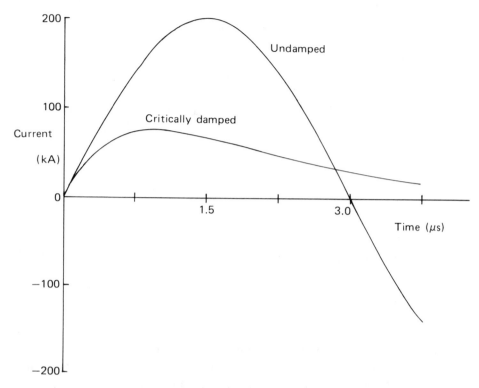

Fig. 2.2 — Discharge circuit waveforms.

obviously includes all stray inductances in the capacitor leads, spark gap, load, and connecting straps. In Fig. 2.3, L_a is the inductance in the resistive load R_1, L_1 and L_2 are the inductances in the connecting straps, and L and R are the lumped values of the remaining inductance and resistance respectively. In terms of 10-cm-wide conductors, $L_1 = L_2 = 10\,\text{nH}$, if the straps are 10 cm long, i.e. if points a, b and c are connections only 10 cm apart on our loop conductor.

In Fig. 2.3 several more components have been added. C_1 is a DC isolating capacitor for the trigger circuit, whole resistors R_s, which are of very high value, hold the trigger electrode of the spark gap at the midplane potential, R_c is a high value charging resistor for C. C_t is the coupling capacitor to the spark gap trigger. This circuit is simplified and lacks some stray capacitances which will be introduced in the next chapter but contains a number of important interference features. A circuit of this kind can generate interference in the following ways

(1) direct radiation as an antenna,

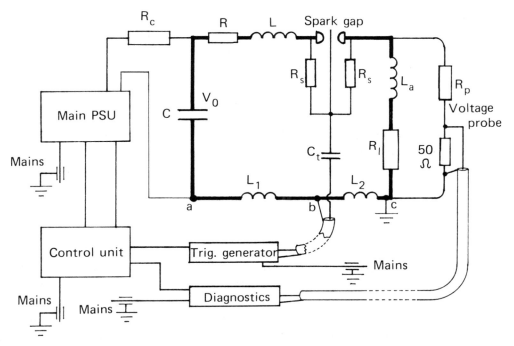

Fig. 2.3 — Pulsed-power circuit configuration.

(2) coupling to external circuits through mutual inductance between the primary discharge loop and an external loop,
(3) high frequency coupling to external circuits through stray capacitance,
(4) coupling to external circuits through multiple ground connections.

The circuit shown has an oscillation frequency of 160 kHz and will radiate at this frequency, acting as a narrow loop antenna about 1 m long. However in this example the antenna dimension is only about 0.0005 wavelengths (λ) and its direct radiation in this mode will be negligible, since electromagnetic theory requires dimensions comparable with 1 λ for efficient radiation into the far field. As such it is a poor example of a direct radiator, as are most low inductance, closed circuits. Were C reduced to 10 pF, assuming it were possible, the circuit would oscillate at 160 MHz, and would radiate most of its stored energy in a few cycles since its dimensions are now about $\lambda/2$. However, the stored energy in this capacitor is only 2 mJ, compared with 2 kJ in the main example.

Coupling of the primary through isolated mutual inductance (2) is not common in the author's experience, because there are likely to be few isolated loops in the vicinity. High currents may be induced in nearby shielding, but most serious effects will occur when the primary inducing circuit and part of the external loop are common, which is case 4.

Coupling through stray capacitance will be considered in detail in the next chapter.

The EMF existing between points a, b, and c in Fig. 2.3 illustrates a most important interference source in pulsed-power technology, and we shall refer to it as the ground loop. The penalty for not controlling this loop can perhaps be compared with that of having very inadequate selectivity in a radio or other tuned receiver.

2.3   THE GROUND LOOP

Consider the circuit of Fig. 2.3, set up in the laboratory for operational use. A safety ground braid will be connected to the circuit. A power supply to charge the capacitor will be required, and this should have, for safety purposes, a ground return as well as the high voltage lead. The power supply unit (PSU) will also have a mains ground lead. The trigger unit to the spark gap should have a coaxial lead to the spark gap with its braid grounded, and it will also have a mains ground. Finally the pulse potential divider to measure the discharge waveform also has a coaxial lead with grounded braid connected to an oscilloscope or digitizer with a grounded mains lead. Along the path, a, b, c there are therefore four ground connections.

The current through L_1 and L_2 is approximately 200 kA, rising in 1.5 μs, so the EMF developed across each ($L dI/dt$) is about 1 kV. The impedance of L_1 or L_2 is ωL, or the voltage divided by the current. Both give a value of about 0.01 Ω. It should now be obvious that EMFs of the order of 1 kV exist between the various ground connections of Fig. 2.3, even though they are attached only 10 cm apart on a massive conductor 10 cm wide. Our concept of grounding needs modification. This large ground-loop EMF is backed by a low source impedance of only 0.01 Ω and is thus capable of driving considerable currents into an external loop. Let us consider such a loop.

Consider the loop formed by the braid of the diagnostic coaxial lead connected at c, continuing through the oscilloscope body to the mains ground, and thence through the mains ground to the trigger generator case and finally back through the trigger coaxial lead to point b. What is the impedance of this loop? In practice the leads considered are likely to trail perhaps 5 m across the laboratory and back, and will probably have an inductance of between 1 and 10 μH. The higher limit has an impedance (ωL) of about 10 Ω. The 1-kV EMF across points b and c will thus drive a current of about 100 A through the braids. This can produce further effects, two of which we will consider, without even worrying about the effects of poor bonding of the cable braids!

Surge currents in the housing of an oscilloscope or digital recorder may cause interference, but good instruments are shielded to a high specification, which makes them suitable for this environment. It is a point that should be checked. The second effect concerns the probe coaxial cable, which will be carrying a diagnostic signal. Since the braid is imperfect the braid current will leak into the coaxial cable, inducing a signal determined by the transfer impedance defined in the previous chapter. At this frequency a typical cable transfer impedance is about 10 mΩ/m. The induced voltage for 100-A current in a 5-m length is thus 5 V. This is larger than many diagnostic signals.

To illustrate the point we have considered numerically a single example of a ground loop, selecting a particular circuit route. Clearly there are more loops in the circuit example chosen, and many in most pulse generator installations. It is the control of ground loops that is most important in reducing interference.

In practice, it is often the identification and control of individual circuit loops or elements that present the problems. The physical mechanisms, as we have seen so far, are relatively simple. In large capacitor-bank installations, the ground loops can be very complex. They may comprise not only the main discharge leads and diagnostic cables, but also involve the whole of the mains wiring of the surrounding building structure. Through metallic contact, or through stray capacitances at high frequencies, the building services (e.g. water and gases) in metallic pipes, the building structure (if metallic) and reinforcing bars in concrete may become involved in the transfer of electromagnetic energy.

Overall control of these factors is necessary in successful reduction of interference pickup. The alternative solution, that of enclosing the complete installation in an unbroken metallic shield (Faraday cage), is usually impracticable. In the limit, all metallic objects within the installation building, or even further afield, must be considered in the light of their ability to facilitate the transfer of interference signals.

Helped by the example, it is hoped to develop this theme to a point where it is apparent that the interference level is a quantity which, though it may be difficult to quantify, is nevertheless built into the system in its design and construction stages. Since installations may be large, complex and closely integrated into their laboratory or building fabric, it follows that reduction of interference levels at a later date may prove difficult and costly. For this reason, it is emphasized that interference merits treatment as a systems concept from the outset, a theme that will be expanded in Chapter 6.

2.4   COUPLING OF THE GROUND LOOP

The ground loop is most clearly illustrated by reference to high pulse powers, as in the example in the last section. However, it is of considerable importance in other areas, for instance in audio frequency amplifiers, in printed circuits, and in integrated circuits, as has already been pointed out. By scaling over a wide range of parameters, and over orders of magnitude, a similar treatment can be used for them as well. Firstly it is necessary to look for the ground loop in the primary circuit which generates the initial EMF: a high current in a low inductance at a relatively high frequency in the example shown. It might be a DC current of 0.1 A in a loop of 10 mΩ resistance, generating 1 mV, which is sufficient to interfere with an operational amplifier. Secondly it should be established whether the magnitude of the EMF is large enough to represent a possible interference problem. If so, then, thirdly, the ground loops into which it may couple must be identified.

At this stage the primary loop will probably have divided into several secondary loops, which themselves may have further subdivided. As the energy transfer process now will almost certainly include distributed stray capacitances (Chapter 6), and mutual inductances, as well as the impedances of the visible leads, further quantification becomes impractical. What is most appropriate at this distance from the source is to identify vulnerable receivers (circuits), and to consider the practicability of breaking loops or of screening receivers.

We have already considered the coupling of a signal from the braid to the inside of a coaxial cable, and the leakage into a screened housing from currents flowing over the surface of the housing, as part of the previous section. If leakage into a screened housing is also taken to include any imperfect screening, such as a badly fitted coaxial plug, then these two mechanisms are the likely end processes by which the interference signal finally enters the receiver. When a signal enters a coaxial cable its route to the receiver is obvious, but the effect of an imperfect shield has almost exactly the same effect as an additional ground loop and can be illustrated by reference to the circuit of Fig. 2.4.

In the figure, A is an amplifier and S the legitimate signal source of impedance R. c–d is the ground connection between amplifier and source S, which may be an imperfect shield or simply a piece of coupling wire. The ground loop current, here assumed to be i, flows between c and d, developing an EMF V. As c is connected to the input to A by impedance R, signal V appears at the amplifier input, and an amplified version will appear as an interference signal at b. Later we shall be advocating the breaking of ground loops, but this idea must be used in its proper context. Breaking the ground loop elsewhere to reduce current i is a good thing in this example, but obviously not by breaking c–d, where we actually require a lower impedance

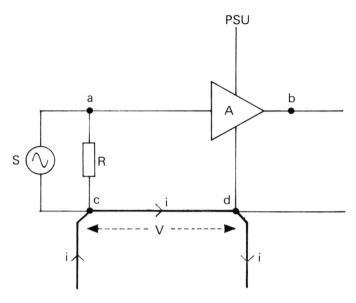

Fig. 2.4 — Amplifier ground loop.

connection or loop. This example of coupling to the effective receiver, though specific, illustrates a common interference problem. Mutual inductance and stray capacitance can also operate, as they do in the earlier stages of the process.

2.5 REDUCTION OF THE GROUND LOOP

The complexity of ground loops should be apparent, even in simple systems, from the previous sections in this chapter. The importance of controlling ground loops, as the most crucial factor in the reduction of near-field interference and spurious triggering, is again stressed. It may be surprising to many people that, properly implemented, it is usually more effective than screening. This is because many interference signals enter the loop close to the primary current generator, where screening is ineffective or impractical. It is quite possible for close-in screening to create an additional ground loop. The current in the braid of a coaxial cable injects a signal into the inside of the cable, as we have already considered. The braid is therefore acting simultaneously as a shield and source of interference.

The ground-loop impedance changes as a function of frequency, and is usually most easily determined at extreme low and high frequencies, but the general aim of treatment should be to effectively break the loops, as far as possible, and to reduce the impedance of those critical loops which cannot be broken. Most intentional ground connections have some function not related to the ground loop they have unintentionally created, and they cannot always be safely disconnected. Therefore emphasis is placed on the term 'effective' breaking of the loop, which means attempting to greatly increase its impedance to reduce the loop current in it, while, preserving the original function of the connection. Specific techniques for increasing the effective impedance of undesirable ground loops will be considered in section 4.4.

The importance of treating interference as a design concept is again emphasized by paying attention to possible loops when the system is initially laid out. The configuration and routing of leads should not be left to chance. Here the engineer/scientist in technical charge can experience considerable difficulties in a large installation. Connection of many varied facilities may be necessary, probably by outside contractors, under the control of site engineers with no knowledge of pulsed or high voltages. Careful organization, education, and supervision are the rule.

2.6　TRANSMISSION LINE AND INDUCTIVE PULSE GENERATORS

To complete this chapter we will briefly consider the two other forms of pulse generator which, like the LCR circuit of section 2.2, can generate pulses of considerable power. The transmission line pulse generator (Lewis and Wells, 1956; Millman and Taub, 1965) is shown in Fig. 2.5 and behaves as a limiting

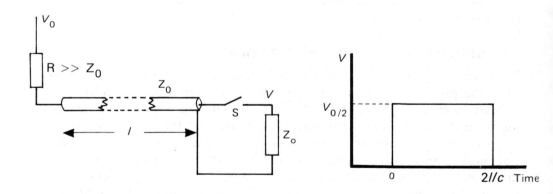

Fig. 2.5 — Transmission line pulse generator.

form of the LCR generator where L and C are the distributed parameters of the line.

The line impedance $Z_0 = (L/C)^{1/2}$ Ω, and when switched into a matched resistive load of this magnitude, a square pulse of amplitude $V_0/2$ and duration twice the electrical length of the line is generated (Fig. 2.5).

This type of generator is best known in radar, but is also associated with fastest (less than 100 ps risetime) and highest power (above 10^{13} W) man-made electrical pulses. Variants of this and the LCR generator include the Marx generator (Fitch, 1971) and the Blumlein line (Blumlein, 1941), and all can generate interference pulses in the ways we have discussed.

Unlike these generators, the inductive generator (Fig. 2.6) relies on the opening rather than the closing of a switch.

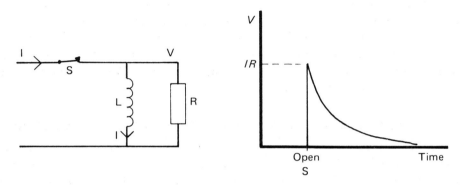

Fig. 2.6 — Inductive pulse generator.

When switch S is closed, a steady current I flows through inductance L, of magnitude determined by the supply circuit impedance. When S is opened a transient EMF IR is generated across L. In practice, if R is large the EMF may be very high, with its risetime determined by the opening characteristic of the switch and by the circuit strays. The source of pulse energy is the energy $\frac{1}{2}LI^2$ originally stored in the inductor.

Though not frequently used as a fast-pulse generator, it is commonly associated with the generation of slow, high energy and current pulses in homopolar and similar rotating electrical machines (Knoepfel, 1970). Though these are also a source of electrical interference, our main interest is that any interrupted circuit is a possible source of transient interference as a result of its inductance, in particular in power lines.

REFERENCEES

Blumlein, A. D. (1941) British patent 589127 Oct. 1941.

Fitch, R. A. (1971) Marx and Marx-like high voltage generators. IEEE *Transactions on Nuclear Science.* NS18, No. 4, 190.

Lewis, I. A. D. & Wells, F. H. (1956) *Millimicrosecond pulse techniques*, Pergamon Press.

Halliday, D. & Resnick, R. (1966) *Physics*, *Parts I and II*, John Wiley.

Knoepful, H. (1970) *Pulsed high magnetic fields*, North-Holland.

Millman, J. & Taub, H. (1965) *Pulse, digital and switching waveforms*, McGraw Hill.

Starling, S. G. (1941) *Electricity and magnetism for degree students*, Longmans, Green and Co.

3

Stray capacitance and high frequency effects

3.1 THE CONCEPT OF STRAY CAPACITANCE

In the previous chapter the concept of a ground loop was introduced, and it was shown that it was caused primarily by the inductive impedance of parts of the circuit normally considered negligible and ignored. In this chapter we consider in a similar way the effects of stray capacitance. This is best known in the field of electronics, where it is often a limit to the high frequency performance of circuits and components, and is associated with close spacings. Stray capacitance exists between all circuit elements and components, and its magnitude is determined by both their sizes and their spacing. Formulae for capacitance and examples are given in section 1.3.

The best-known effect of stray capacitance in electronic circuits is as an

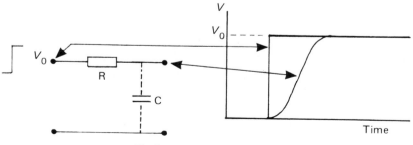

Fig. 3.1 — Shunt capacitance.

effective shunting impedance (Fig. 3.1), progressively attenuating the input signal from a source of finite impedance as the frequency increases. It is usually undesirable, since it limits high frequency response, but can often be used for this purpose by deliberately introducing capacitance when fast transients are to be decoupled. The main concern of stray capacitance in high voltage pulsed systems is as a means of transfer of energy from a conductor undergoing a high rate of change of potential to an adjacent conductor designed to operate at low potential. As such it has some analogy with the Miller effect in electronics (Millman and Taub, 1965), a feedback mechanism which can cause instability and oscillation. However, its main effects for our consideraation are signals causing spurious triggering and obscuring diagnostic waveforms.

Since stray capacitance is determined by both the size and spacing of conductors, it is a fully three-dimensional effect and in rigorous form requires the solution of Maxwell's equations in three dimensions. In our study of interference it is also essentially a concept of the empty space in a system, and may therefore be doubly difficult to visualize. At high frequencies it may actually constitute part of a ground loop, even though it is not visible like a metallic conductor. Though invisible, at high rates of change of potential it will not go away!

In the next section of this chapter we will consider values of capacitance likely to be found in practice, and in the third section the magnitudes of currents resulting from the strays. The effect will obviously increase with increasing frequency and with increasing associated potential. In the limits of high frequency, the finite time of propagation of the pulse must be considered, when the effects of capacitance and inductance merge into distributed impedance effects. These will be considered briefly in this chapter, and in more detail in Chapter 5.

3.2 MAGNITUDE OF STRAY CAPACITANCES

Although the estimation of stray capacitance values in a complex, three-dimensional system of laboratory size may initially seem daunting, it can be considerably simplified in practice. Most shapes can be treated as a collection of one or more of the basic spherical, cylindrical, rectangular plate, or coaxial configurations whose capacitances are easily calculated. In fact the essential skill is in visualizing the simplest forms, whose calculated capacitances differ negligibly from those of the critical parts of the actual system. The writer has been greatly influenced by the pioneering, but largely unpublished, work of J. C. Martin and his group at AWE Aldermaston on the design and operation of high power Marx generators. Here control of the complex stray capacitances between components is vital to successful triggering and erection of the Marx.

Many leads in an electrical system will be directly grounded. Many more will be effectively grounded with respect to fast transients, though they may actually be operating at low or high DC potentials, or at mains voltage. What this means is that they have a high capacitance to ground, because they are in a grounded conduit, lie against a metal chassis, are in a long bundle with grounded leads, or connect to a component with a high ground capacitance. In this last category are most mains leads, which usually have a high capacitance to the building ground via conduit and ground wires and to electrical equipment via the high interwinding capacitances in mains transformers. This is why the common strategy of breaking the ground wire in the mains lead to reduce transient interference on oscilloscopes seldom works, but often results in electric shock from the chassis. It is often important to identify leads which are transiently grounded by stray capacitance, both for elimination and sometimes to use them to shield vulnerable leads.

Table 1.2 shows the capacitance, with air dielectric, of a number of common shapes, with typical or illustrative dimensions. In the table, capacitances are shown per metre length, except for concentric spheres, while the other two spatial dimensions are shown as a ratio (see Table 1.1). The majority of structural shapes, excluding long wires, which are met in practice have linear dimensions of the same order of magnitude as the separation from their neighbours.

Three important deductions may be made from the formulae and from these examples:

(1) Low capacitances of a few picofarads are characteristic only of small electrodes, of linear dimensions not more than a few millimetres and with separations exceeding 100 mm.
(2) Capacitances of tens of picofarads are typical of the majority of shapes whose linear dimensions and spacings are roughly equal and are about 100 mm. Similar capacitances exist in typical transmission lines and between closely spaced wires for lengths of 1 m. The capacitance in these cases is a slowly varying function of spacing or diameter.
(3) Large capacitances, 1 nF or more, are associated with electrodes of linear dimensions and spacings measured in metres, or, in the case of small systems, where the electrodes have linear dimensions in two directions of about 100 mm with close spacings of 1 mm.

It is hoped that we have demonstrated that a capacitance (in air) of between 10 and 50 pF is characteristic of most shapes in laboratory-bench-sized equipment.

Two further comments are appropriate to these figures. Firstly they can be scaled to much larger or smaller systems where the ratio of one dimension to spacing remains similar, and the third dimension, where appropriate, increases or decreases. Secondly, the small range of capacitance met shows that it is insensitive to fine details of shape, so that it is relatively easy to break a complex shape into one or more of the simple basic shapes illustrated. It may be suggested that Maxwell's equations have, in this instance, been kinder to us!

Clearly, when estimating strays in this way, only near-neighbour conductors should be considered. If the capacitance between two conductors is being examined in a system where a third conductor effectively shields one from the other, a two-stage interaction must be considered. The effective capacitance will depend critically on the status of the third conductor, whether it is grounded, or floating, for example. In minimizing the effects of stray capacitance, the interpretive skill of the diagnostician is thus very important. In one instance, the interposition of a grounded screen may eliminate the effect of an undesirable stray, but in another case the increase in the stray resulting from so doing may cause an undesirable ground current. Increasing the lead spacing may be the better solution in the latter case, or reduction of the wire diameter, though Tables 1.1 and 1.2 show that the actual reduction in the stray will be small.

3.3   CURRENTS INDUCED BY STRAY CAPACITANCE AT HIGH FREQUENCY

At a frequency of 1 MHz the impedance of a capacitor of 10 pF is given by:

$$1/\omega C \simeq 1.5 \times 10^4 \, \Omega$$

This is a relatively high impedance, but is nevertheless low enough to couple appreciable energy even into low impedance circuits of 50 Ω. A 1-MHz signal of 1 kV applied to a 10 pF capacitor coupled to a 50 Ω resistor will result in a potential of approximately 3 V across the latter. These figures may therefore be taken as a rough criterion for the frequency at which strays start to become important in a 1-kV system, using TTL-voltage electronics at low impedance, and may be scaled in a linear fashion for systems with different parameters.

Let us consider again the capacitor discharge circuikt of Fig. 2.3, reproduced as Fig. 3.2 with the addition of two stray capacitances, namely, 10 pF from the switch side of the load to the ground side, and 1 pF across the load-voltage monitor resistor. The addition of two strays only is a considerable simplification of a practical problem, but the capacitance values used are similar to those in a real system.

Suppose, in Fig 3.2 that a 50-kV-amplitude, 10-ns-risetime trigger pulse is applied to the trigger pin, from a 50-Ω cable, 50 Ω therefore represents the source impedance, and 1 kA the maximum trigger current attainable.

Whether a current of this magnitude actually flows depends on the transient impedance in the circuit.

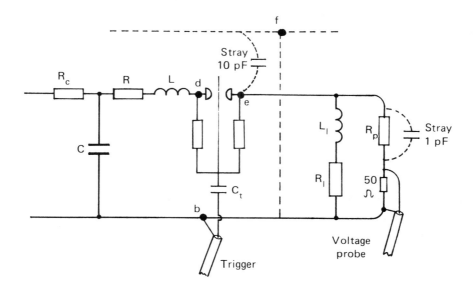

Fig. 3.2 — Stray capacitance in a pulse circuit.

Let us suppose, for simplicity, that the trigger electrode rapidly breaks down to the spark gap electrode on the load side and establishes a low impedance in a time of the order of 10 ns. Let us also suppose that the load remains open-circuit for this period of time, although it should have sufficient stray capacitance (100 pF) to pass the initial spark gap breakdown current. Point e will rise in potential to approach 50 kV in 10 ns. The maximum current which will then flow through the 10-pF stray capacitance to point f is given by:

$$\frac{C\delta V}{\delta t} \simeq 50\,A$$

Whether this magnitude of current will actually flow depends on the external impedance between points f and b. It will if the impedance is represented by an inductance of 1 μH or less. A current of this magnitude is similar to that of the ground-loop current discussed in Chapter 2, and similarly a likely source of interference.

If the external impedance between points f and b is equivalent to 10 µH or more, the potential at f will tend to follow that of e rather than remain at the potential of b; f will rise in potential by tens of kilovolts with respect to b during the period of interest. The previous ground-loop current will be much reduced, but there may be other undesirable effects, namely:

(a) Electrical breakdown and sparking external to the main circuit, a further source of interference.
(b) Electric shock hazards, which may be remote from the capacitor bank.

An alternative way of determining the order of magnitude of loop currents is by a crude application of Ohm's law, in which reactances are replaced by an ohmic resistance of the same magnitude. Phase shifts in potential and current, normally shown by a negative sign for capacitative reactance and a positive sign for inductive reactance, are ignored. This method usually works well, either because only an order of magnitude estimate is necessary, or because the reactive impedance is predominant or negligible.

If in the same circuit, capacitative and inductive reactances of strays are of similar magnitude, there will be a resonance condition in which phase factors cannot be ignored. Either a detailed circuit analysis will be necessary or one of the strays may be artificially altered to move well away from resonance.

In a pulse circuit in which the signal risetime is 10 ns, the associated high frequency bandwidth limit is approximately 30 MHz. The impedance of 10 pF is $1/\omega C \simeq 500\ \Omega$, and the impedance of 1 µH is $\omega L \simeq 200\ \Omega$ at 30 MHz.

A risetime of 10 ns is characteristic of many trigger circuits, and as such it is used in these illustrations. In a circuit containing the above impedances, and a pulse source of 50 Ω, the latter can be considered as a constant voltage source, and the approximate magnitude of the external loop current can be obtained by dividing the voltage by the appropriate loop impedance. These figures illustrate order of magnitude calculations in simple cases. In practice the circuits usually consist of both types of reactances, in combination with resistance, but the use of discrete component impedances is very valuable, because it often enables a quick elimination process to be used in simplifying the analysis of more complex circuits. Simple impedance estimation also illustrates how ground-loop currents at 30 MHz frequency can be decreased from 100 A with 1 µH inductance to 1 A if the ground-loop inductance can be artificially increased to 100 µH. This forms the basis of one form of ground-loop isolation to be described later.

Also in Fig. 3.2, a small, but typical, stray capacitance of 1 pF is shown shunting the high impedance side of a voltage monitor designed to measure the waveform across the load. If it is intended to attenuate a 20-kV amplitude waveform to 10 V, to feed through coaxial cable to an oscilloscope, the monitor resistance should be 100 kΩ. The impedance of 1 pF at 30 MHz is approximately 5 kΩ, and at 1 MHz approximately 150 kΩ.

As shown, the attenuator will show a reasonable approximation to the correct waveform at 1-MHz frequency, and an accurate waveform at 100 kH. However at 30-MHz frequency (the main component of our trigger pulses), signals will displayed an order of magnitude larger than the calibrated value, apart from any phase shifts. The trigger pulse is probably unwanted on the display, and is actually at a level which may damage the semiconductor circuits of the recording system. Having demonstrated the undesirable effect of this stray capacitance in the interference context, possible direct solutions to the problem are as follows:

(a) Use lower resistances, if this does not appreciably load the circuit.
(b) Shunt the lower end of the potential divider with a capacitance so that the time constants of the upper and lower sections are equal.
(c) Use a capacitative divider, though this and (b) may introduce problems of calibration.

We have already established that the capacitance between coaxial and between parallel conductors is a logarithmic function, resulting in a small range of capacitance, 10–100 pF, for a large range of configurations of small laboratory size. The reader may check that the small capacitance range results from the fact that, as objects in an actual system are brought closer together, their surface areas must necessarily be reduced to enable them to fit in. It also follows that it is difficult in practice to reduce direct strays much below 10 pF by increasing the spacing in normal laboratory-sized systems.

As a consequence, at a frequency of 30 MHz, all metal components of the order of 1 m^2 in area and several metres away from the capacitor bank present an impedance of the order of 1000 Ω to the bank circuits. They can therefore act as efficient means of transfer of electrical energy to circuits to which they themselves are directly or indirectly connected. Clearly these latter circuits, which usually include conduits and mains wiring, assume importance in interference technology.

3.4   EFFECTS AT VERY HIGH FREQUENCIES (ABOVE 50 MHz)

As discussed in the previous section, at a frequency of about 30 MHz the impedance of both a typical stray capacitance (10 pF) and lead inductance (1 µH) are of a similar magnitude about 300 Ω within a factor of 2. This is close to the impedance of free space (377 Ω) and within the order of magnitude of that of typical transmission lines. The reader may check if this is a coincidence or a fundamental property!

In laboratory-sized systems this frequency may be taken as marking a change from treating the system as one of lumped parameters to treating it as one of distributed parameters. The half-wavelength of this frequency is 5 m, just the size of a small laboratory, and our choice of 10 ns and 30 MHz is thus no coincidence! It also means that here we must anticipate both lumped and distributed parameter effects together.

Beyond 50 MHz there is an important change of emphasis towards distributed parameters, and as such this will be considered in more detail in a later chapter. It is important to remember, however, that this distinction has been applied to a particular technology and system size, with which the writer is most familiar. The frequency may seem low to a microwave or integrated circuit engineer or to a printed circuit board designer, but by linearly scaling the frequency and typical dimension, e.g. to 1 GHz and 150 mm, most of the discussion in this chapter can be seen to be equally relevant to the smaller systems. Care must be taken when scaling in this way to check in which direction the strays also scale. Smaller systems will be considered in a later chapter.

REFERENCE

Millman, J. & Taub, H. (1965) *Pulse, digital, and switching waveforms.* McGraw Hill Book Co.

4

Shielding and reduction of pickup

4.1 REMOVAL OR REDUCTION AT SOURCE

Reduction of interference is often considered in terms of the introduction of a screen between source and receiver. We have tried to emphasize it in terms of generation and coupling processes, with the control of these as the primary method of reduction, and the use of a screened room or enclosure as a possible solution only when the other methods have failed.

In the author's experience, reduction of interference at source is usually, in the long term, the easiest and most cost-effective solution, but at the same time the most difficult to persuade people to implement. The reason is probably that there is the realization of an immediate cost and a failure to realize that interference is the norm. In the previous chapters it has been demonstrated how unwanted signals are coupled into circuits through finite, but often ignored, impedances. That the process has been treated through pulsed-power technology is just one way of dealing with a much wider ranging problem. Most of the principles of shielding were familiar to radio and radar engineers before the era of transistors, nuclear EMP, and digital systems, an excellent treatment being given by Zepler (1945). To the author there is the appearance of a large gap in time before they have been transferred to, or reinvented in, these newer fields. Although it is obviously better to remove interference at the source, the problem is most frequently ignored until interference signals distort diagnostic waveforms or cause malfunctions. At this stage, adequate shielding or decoupling of the source, particularly in large installations may be impracticable, and the problem must be solved in the diagnostics. A further difficulty here is that the system designer and the diagnostician may be different persons, and may even be under different administration. If it is a truism that many interference problems are introduced in the design, or as a result of the method of construction, the solution is obvious. If interference is removed at source, all users will benefit, otherwise each may have to solve a separate shielding problem.

Commercial high quality shielded rooms are frequently used in medium- or large-sized installations. These, and many smaller available enclosures used with electronic equipment are capable of attenuation levels as high as 100 dB, provided associated leads are correctly interfaced. This will be considered in detail later in this chapter, for it is crucial in determining whether a shielded enclosure works. Proper screening in large systems can be difficult and expensive to implement because it usually needs to be complete. It therefore involves large areas of metal sheet, with edges bonded together, and a means of bringing electrical leads, but not interference, through the sheets. Therefore we will first consider the means of reduction at the source by controlling the circuit strays whose concepts and magnitudes were outlined in the previous chapters.

4.2 DISCHARGE CIRCUIT INDUCTANCE

Sometimes, reduction of all, or part, of the main circuit in a typical discharge circuit will reduce the interference current injected into a ground or other circuit loop. Reduction of inductance in one part of the circuit will often simply reduce the voltage drop across it and hence the EMF available to inject current into the ground loop. In general, reduction of inductance will also reduce mutual inductance and decrease induced interference EMFs.

Good practice therefore suggests low inductance as a rule, with spacings and positioning for minimum mutual inductances.

In many pulse circuits the foregoing statements about reducing inductance may seem incompatible where the circuit inductance magnitude is critical in determining the pulse waveshape. However, the anomaly can be removed by identifying parts of the circuit where the high inductive EMF or mutual inductance is ineffective in coupling out an interference signal, and separating them from the critical, interference-producing loops. These latter may then be reduced while maintaining the overall inductance magnitude.

As an example, the problem may occur in the flashtube capacitor banks of a pulsed glass-laser system. In this instance, the laser (flashtube) modules are likely to be sited some distance from the capacitor banks, to which they will be connected by long leads. At the same time, a relatively high circuit inductance may be required to determine the duration of the discharge waveform. Incorporating the inductance in the long leads may be an obvious and simple solution, but it is one that is most likely to produce large ground loops and cause interference. A better solution is to use heavily braided coaxial cable for the long leads, which gives both screening and minimum loop inductance, and to site separate, compact inductors close to the capacitors.

4.3   REDUCTION OF STRAY CAPACITANCE

Reduction of stray capacitance by reduction of electrode size and increase in spacing is normally highly desirable, though there are practical limits discussed in Chapter 3. It is important to remember that the spacing is a three-dimensional quantity and increase in spacing in one direction may not be of value if there is a corresponding reduction in another. An indirect way of reducing a stray capacitance is by shielding as illustrated in Fig. 4.1, where (a)

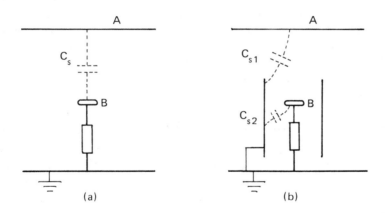

Fig. 4.1 — Shielding of stray capacitance.

shows the stray C_s between plane A and a component B. Fitting a grounded shield round B, as in Fig. 4.1(b), considerably reduces the magnitude of C_s by intercepting the electrostatic field lines. In doing so it introduces additional capacitances C_{s1} and C_{s2}, both larger than the original C_s, and although this will not usually matter, in some cases the higher ground-loop currents resulting from the higher overall capacitance may cause worse effects than the original stray. The technique is well-known in the design of high frequency voltage dividers, where the increased capacitive loading of the circuit is offset by a frequency-stable division ratio.

While discussing reduction of stray capacitance we will consider a common and related effect, an undesirable ringing common to trigger and other drive circuits. It is caused by the presence of stray inductance and capacitance in the signal leads, and produces an oscillation when excited by a fast-rising pulse. Well-known in the era of vacuum valves (tubes), the solution is still the same, either to reduce the strays so that the ringing frequency is above the response of the system, or, if this is not possible, to introduce enough series resistance to the lead to critically damp the oscillation.

If such oscillating circuits have long leads they will radiate interference, and critically damping them will considerably reduce the energy they radiate, with little reduction in the risetime response. It is a simple, but very important, technique, and though less well known in the pulsed power field, it is now used in all car ignition systems and in relay, thyristor, and general contact-spark suppression. Not only is interference reduced, but so is contact damage.

As mentioned in the last chapter, one of the common effects of stray capacitance is as circuit loading, which may limit the high frequency response. This is usually undesirable, but there are instances where the interference signal is at the higher frequency, and this attenutation effect can be used to advantage. Here artificial increase of the stray can be used to preferentially attenuate the interference.

4.4 PRACTICAL REDUCTION OF GROUND LOOPS

In large or complex installations, and particularly in pulsed-power systems, breaking the ground loops is usually the first and most important means of interference reduction. The removal of unnecessary metallic connections by spacing or by introduction of insulating sheet is fairly obvious, for example, where capacitors or part of the discharge circuit rest on metallic building structural members or touch a laboratory access cage. Direct breaking of the ground loops in many instances is not possible, but indirect breaking can often be achieved by the introduction of a high impedance, provided it does not interfere with the normal function of the ground lead. We will illustrate the problem, firstly by considering a number of connections to a typical pulse-power system which give rise to multiple ground loops, and then by suggesting possible ways of decoupling them. Connections may be divided up according to power and function as follows:

(a) Leads at high voltage carrying appreciable DC power, e.g. PSU output leads.
(b) Leads carrying fast pulses, such as trigger pulses:

(i) those carrying high pulsed powers (e.g. 10^6 W),

(ii) those carrying low powers (e.g. 1 W).

(c) Leads carrying mains power within the installation:

   (i) high mains powers (above 1 kV A), e.g. large high voltage power supplies, air conditioning, etc.,
   (ii) Low mains powers (less than 1 kV A), e.g. small PSUs, lighting, actuators, etc.

   Leads in category (c) are assumed not to connect directly to the discharge circuits, but to be indirectly close-coupled by strays, and may carry transient displacement currents.
(d) Leads carrying low level, low frequency power or signals, e.g. remote status monitoring leads, safety interlocks, communications, etc.
(e) Critical transient diagnostic monitor leads carrying pulsed (high frequency) signals of various powers.
(f) Any and every metallic connection to the system which exists for any reason whatsoever but which is not a deliberate electrical connection in the previous categories. This may include, for instance, metal plumbing and compressed air pipes, old conduit, a metal floor on which the system stands, building stanchions to which the racks of a capacitor bank have been bolted, etc.

These categories are not mutually exclusive and are intended to facilitate a breakdown of the types of leads according to the decoupling which is most appropriate. Next we will consider decoupling techniques which can be used, their advantages and disadvantages.

The following methods can be used to reduce the ground loop:

(1) Disconnection of unnecessary electrical leads.
(2) Insulation of the system metal framework from the floor and from the building structure.
(3) Replacement of metal service pipes to the system by insulating materials.
(4) Replacement of electrical leads which provide slow-operating control functions by non-electrical actuation, e.g. rotating, insulating shafts, compressed air, etc.
(5) Use of pulse or RF transformers with low primary-to-secondary capacitance for the transmission of low power pulses and RF.
(6) Use of electro-optic links to replace signal and control leads.
(7) Introduction of high resistance or inductance into power or control

lines, provided that the high impedance introduced into the ground loop does not impede the normal function.

(7a) Coiling of power and coaxial signal leads into an inductance as a special case of (7).

(8) General separation of the system from surrounding metalwork using space, insulating sheets, and blocks of insulation where appropriate. In doing this all safety (mains) ground connections must be maintained, as this is often a legal as well as an overriding safety requirement.

(9) Finally, during design and installation, care in the circuit and system layout, with the primary aim of eliminating and reducing the ground loops. Included here are special concepts such as the dual-level grounding introduced on pulsed laser systems at Lawrence Livermore Laboratory, California (Gagnon, 1975). Here the ground circuits of the pulsed-power discharges and of the control systems were kept separate and only linked at controlled places.

None of the foregoing should, under any circumstances, interfere with the provision of an overall ground connection to the system which provides a low impedance path at DC and mains frequency. The general relation between the types of leads in the first list and the decoupling techniques in the second should be apparent, but in the rest of this section we will consider them in more detail. It should by now be clear that, in any decoupling technique, the effect of the inevitable stray capacitance remaining must also be considered (see Chapter 3).

Non-electrical actuation is frequently used in larger installations as a means of reducing electrical leads, and a wide range of reliable compressed air and hydraulic components with electrical interfaces are available. The firing and safety dump switches of a high current electromagnetic launcher described by Seddon and Thornton (1988b) were operated in this way.

Introduction of series resistance with the stated provisos is particularly useful in power supply leads which are not carrying high powers. It is a simple technique, one frequently used by the author, and relatively easily incorporated as the system is built. When, later, inevitable interference signals are discovered, all such leads can be immediately eliminated from guilt, and the search considerably narrowed! In the case of power leads, it is wise to decouple the ground return lead as well. It is often tempting to eliminate this lead and rely on some other return path, but, though the elimination is good for interference reduction, it can be dangerous in the case of high voltage power supplies if the other path becomes disconnected without reference to the supply.

Where the DC current is so large that series resistance is not acceptable, an inductance may be introduced. Table 4.1 shows the impedance of

Table 4.1 — Impedance of inductors

	100 kHz	1 MHz	10 MHz	100 MHz
1 μH	0.6 Ω	6 Ω	60 Ω	600 Ω
10 μH	6 Ω	60 Ω	600 Ω	6 kΩ
100 μH	60 Ω	600 Ω	6 kΩ	60 kΩ

representative inductances at various frequencies. For instance the impedance of 100 μH at 100 kHz is 60 Ω, and will increase that of a typical ground loop of 1 μH by two orders of magnitude. At higher frequencies, even lower inductances are valuable. The technique is particularly useful and, when used in conjunction with decoupling capacitors, forms the basis of filters. It is a means of introducing leads into shielded enclosures, as will be considered in Chapter 8.

Decoupling by inductive isolation is a particularly valuable means of breaking ground loops which are carrying considerable DC or mains power. An example is mains leads of several KVA power rating, because the three-core lead can easily be coiled into a single layer inductance of 100 μH. The integrity of the normal mains ground is preserved by this technique. It has been used for many years by J. C. Martin and his group at AWE, and was used on the pulsed high current electron beam machine EROS, and on high power fast-pulse Nd-glass and CO_2 lasers. In the case of the lasers it was particularly useful in reducing the effects of trigger transients.

It is a simple and cheap technique for breaking the ground loop of diagnostic oscilloscope mains leads. The three-core mains lead is simply wound on an insulating former 7–10 cm in diameter and 30–50 cm long. It should be wound as a single layer to reduce stray capacitance, for reasons that should become apparent in the next chapter. The inductance, about 100 μH, breaks the ground loop very effectively in the 100 kHz–100 MHz frequency range at least. The increased mains voltage drop, and cable heating is usually insignificant, but should be checked.

The identical technique is commonly used in the case of coaxial signal leads which are part of ground loops. In this case the inductance can be considerably increased by coiling round a large ferrite toroid. A large inductance may be necessary here if lower frequency leakage through the cable braid is distorting a diagnostic waveshape.

A disadvantage of inductive isolators is their necessarily large size and awkward positioning, because they will consist of a single-layer coil some 30 cm in length in order to accommodate the cable with minimum stray capacitance between the ends. They therefore protrude from otherwise neat racks and screened enclosures, are vulnerable to collision and are unpopular with facility engineers.

The availability of cheap optoelectronic isolators greatly facilitates the use of digital control in large installations in which electrical interference is present. In conjunction with the fibre optics, they can be used to completely isolate low power circuits over many metres of spacing. There is a wide range of applications, from monitoring safety interlock circuits to triggering sophisticated diagnostic equipment with sub-nanosecond risetimes. Both digital and analogue information can be transmitted. In large pulsed-power installations, of which the Lawrence Livermore Laboratory SHIVA laser is an early example (Gilmartin *et al.* 1975), opto-isolators of over 10 kV were used and were vital in microprocessor control of all parts of the system.

In opto-isolators, power is normally required by both transmitter and receiver. Since optoelectronic equipment operates at low voltage, it is itself susceptible to interference, and components must be well shielded. Its power requirement should therefore be regarded as an Achilles' heel, and the leads should be extremely well shielded, or batteries used. As power requirements are small they may be taken from existing supplies in nearby parts of the system.

When lower power circuits can be decoupled by the introduction of series resistance, the ground-loop current can be considerably reduced. However, there may still exist an appreciable stray capacitance across this resistance, which can be reduced by breaking down the resistance into a number of series elements.

These techniques vary from the simple and obvious to more sophisticated methods whose cost-effectiveness may be less apparent. Insulation of the framework (2) of a large installation may be difficult, but the arguments with the construction engineers in order to implement it may well be worth winning, for it is you, not they, who will be left afterwards to deal with the interference!

The replacement of metal pipes by plastic ones (3), and the use of non-electric actuators (4), are also obvious. Clearly suitability, for instance of pressure lines and for containment of toxic liquids, must be considered.

The use of electro-optic isolation and fibre-optic links (FOL) is now extensive and is a powerful interference-reducing technique. It is particularly suited to diagnostic signal links, and to digital control systems. Through FOLs, computer bus lines can be fed round large installations in the presence of interference signals. The important reservation in the use of electro-optics has already been mentioned. Both the drive and the receiver ends of the device usually consist of sensitive electronic circuitry, which themselves are interference-sensitive. Rigorous shielding, as in most commercial units, is vital, or more interference will be introduced than would be by the electrical link it is replacing.

4.5 SHIELDING

As shielding is usually the first solution considered in the reduction of interference, we have deliberately considered other solutions first in an attempt to bring it into the context of one among a number of others. Partly this helps to emphasize the idea of treating interference at source. However, it must be realized that there are many cases where interference problems cannot be treated in this way because the source is remote or otherwise outside user control. In emphasizing control at source, the author hopes he will be excused by those not able to control the primary source, in particular those who shield aircraft and those involved with lightning protection. Here shielding may be crucial.

The concept of shielding is based on the conclusion of the Faraday ice pail experiment, that there is no charge on the inside of a closed, hollow conductor. Extending this concept to varying electromagnetic fields requires that the container walls be of such thickness, electrical conductivity, and permeability that there is negligible leakage of field through the walls. In practice this criterion is not usually difficult to achieve with metal sheet, though at audio frequencies magnetic fields will penetrate thin sheet. The primary problem in shielding is caused by the imperfections in the walls resulting from joints, holes, doors, windows, and leads passing through them. It is to these that we will devote most attention.

Before considering these details, however, it should always be remembered that the aim of the shield is to divide space into two parts, one containing the source and the other the receiver. If this is adequately done in the first instance, it is then possible to move to the next stage, which is to consider the leads which must pass through the shield. In doing this it is logical to introduce an additional concept, which is very important in dealing with complex shielding problems, such as occur in aircraft and vehicles. It is the topological approach (Tesche, 1978; Lee, 1986). The topological decomposition of a system is performed (Fig. 4.2) by breaking down the system into a series of enclosed shells, where each shell can be identified as a specific enclosure, for instance, the outer skin, an internal cabin, an enclosed cable loom, a piece of electronic equipment, a shielded enclosure, and so on. It is important that the enclosures be correctly identified in their relationships: alongside, e.g. V1.1, V1.2, V1.3, etc., or one inside the other, e.g. V1.1, V2.1, V3.1, etc. Next the leads and cables as they traverse the system and pass through shells are identified and the imperfections and leakage paths through the shells. In this way the passage of an interference signal

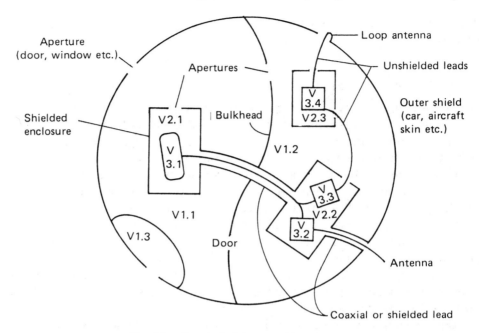

Fig. 4.2 — Topological decomposition of a system.

from the outside to some point inside can be tracked. If it can be shown that the signal, in passing one level of shell enclosing the receiver, is attenuated to a safe level, analysis through further inner shells is unnecessary. Care must be taken to check that there are not direct routes which bypass the shells, and it should be remembered that the system is reciprocal, and source and receiver can be interchanged if the system elements are all linear in response.

In the systems and components that we shall consider, a simplified topological approach is implicit. This can be extended to much larger and complex systems such as aircraft, as in the above references, but is likely to require an extensive analytical treatment, or simulation experiments, or both. The concept of a completely enclosing, conducting shell should always be in mind, because it is the ideal to which practical implementation should always aspire. Any imperfect part may transmit an interference signal, and in the remainder of this section we shall consider practical systems and criteria.

A coaxial cable may be connected to a screened room to transmit a diagnostic signal from an external transducer to an internal recorder. The inside of the coaxial cable may be considered as an extension of the inside volume of the screened room, the coaxial braid being the extension of the metal wall. The coaxial cable must pass through a hole in the wall, which will therefore break the integrity of shielding. If the braid is securely bonded to the metal wall at the hole (Fig. 4.3(a), integrity is maintained.

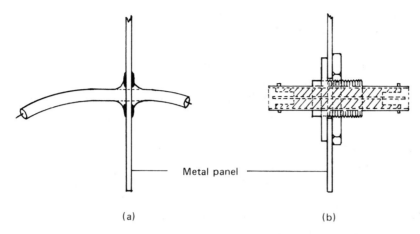

Fig. 4.3 — Shield integrity: (a) solder bond, (b) bulkhead fitting.

In practice, opening out and soldering cable braids is inconvenient, and a better and more flexible solution is to bolt on standard coaxial bulkhead couplings (Fig. 4.3(b)), into which cables are plugged on either side. That the need for secure bonding is frequently unknown, or forgotten, is shown by the number of cables seen simply pushed through holes drilled into expensive shielded rooms. In this last instance the braid may act as an efficient antenna to pick up interference outside and reradiate it inside. It can conduct a large ground-loop current inside, while, if bonded, such a current will be conducted to the outside skin of the room. Later we hope to extend this latter concept further to double screening.

So far we have considered screening in terms of surrounding a receiver, but reciprocity shows that the source can equally well be shielded, and often with greater effect. If complete electrical shielding of the interference source is relatively easy, and compatible with access and servicing, it should be implemented. It may render elaborate shielding of the diagnostics unnecessary, allowing greater flexibility in the use of diagnostic equipment. Only one shield is required for the source; each diagnostic device may require separate shielding. As already pointed out, shielding is easier to implement at the outset of construction of a system. Very sensitive diagnostics may require maximum shielding of both source and recording systems. For effective shielding the metallic cover must be complete. The appropriate techniques follow closely those used in conventional RF and microwave technology. Joints in shielding panels should ideally be soldered or welded, or, if they are bolted, they should overlap by at least $0.1\,\lambda$, and be bolted at intervals of not more than $0.5\,\lambda$, where λ is the wavelength of the highest frequency signal to be shielded.

Ground-loop currents involving the shielded enclosure should obviously be kept to a minimum, and this refers not only to magnitude, but also to the area of surface carrying currents. All leads associated with the enclosure should therefore be grouped at a single panel for connection and entry to the enclosure. This will reduce ground-loop circulating currents in the skin of the enclosure. For the same reason the shielded room should ideally be insulated from building services and structural members, including, if possible, the floor. Mains leads to a shielded enclosure should pass through an efficient low-pass filter at the shield; a range of commercial devices are available to suit the required power rating. As many of these are installed with the mains conduit bonded to the filter case and the shielded wall, the author prefers, for pulsed-power work, to further decouple the ground line. This is achieved, as already described, by simply coiling the mains and ground lead, and will reduce any pulsed currents in the shield skin from this source. It should be remembered that some users may need to achieve a higher level of attenuation than the 100 dB of a good quality screened room. However, in some pulsed-power work it is sufficient to decouple the mains by an inductive isolator and pass the mains through a gland in the shield wall which is both a feedthrough capacitor and a cutoff waveguide. It will be described later in this chapter.

4.6 SINGLE AND DOUBLE SHIELDING

Commercial shielded rooms for RF purposes are usually of modular construction so that a range of sizes can be accommodated. They consist of plain metal panels or laminated ones, e.g. chipboard sandwiched between two metal panels. Rigid metal frames securely clamp the panels together along their edges using conducting gaskets to give a continuous and unbroken electrical seal. Double-panelled door seals with twin lines of continuous spring metal fingers, which join door to frame in two lines are fitted round all four edges. Fig. 4.4 shows the method of construction of a commercial enclosure giving 100 dB attenuation over a wide frequency range.

This method is a mixture of double and single screening, and may serve to illustrate how the enclosure has been derived from the early models which used two layers of chicken mesh. A mesh provides an electromagnetic shield, and if the mesh crossings are bonded, as in galvanized mesh or in expanded metal, an attenuation of about 40 dB is achievable. It works up to the frequency where the wavelength approaches 0.2 of the mesh size, beyond which an appreciable signal will diffract through the hole. A second mesh, separated by a spacing of at least five times the mesh size will give a further attenuation of 40 dB, or up to about 80 dB total. Separate doors in each mesh frame were used to maintain this attenuation. It should be apparent that the type of shielded room illustrated in Fig. 4.4 uses double screening where

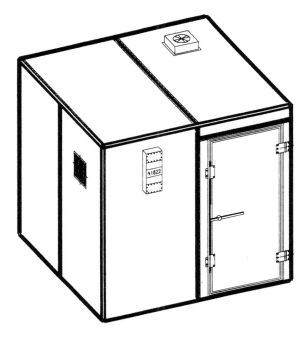

Series 81 modular shielded enclosure

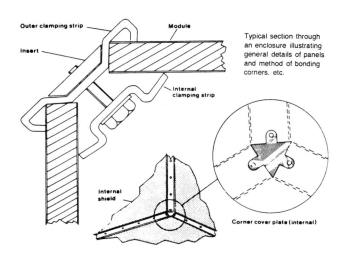

Outer clamping strip

Insert

Module

Internal
clamping strip

Typical section through
an enclosure illustrating
general details of panels
and method of bonding
corners, etc.

Internal
shield

Corner cover plate (internal)

Courtesy of Ray Proof Ltd.

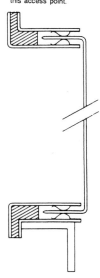

Details of form of knife–
edge door with beryllium
copper finger strips to
maintain RF integrity at
this access point.

Fig. 4.4 — Construction of a shielded room.

there are join weaknesses, e.g. door edges, but single or simple laminated panels elsewhere to reduce costs. Woven mesh alone is not a suitable screen because there is no positive electrical bond at the weave crossing points.

The concept of double screening can be particularly cost-effective when a flexible, or ventilated shield is required. Braids can easily be threaded over coaxial cables to compensate for leakage through the first braid. The outer braid should be insulated along its length from the inner to reduce coupling even further. Undesirable circulating currents should be confined to the outer braid only, but it is not always clear how the ends of the outer should be connected for optimum shielding (Baker *et al.*, 1970).

At low frequencies the skin effect limits the shielding efficiency of thin metal sheet, and penetration of the magnetic field may occur. In large, permanent installations it is practicable to make the room from a single screen of thick steel sheets with carefully welded joints. The large shielded room in the Electromagnetic Compatibility Centre at British Eurospace, Filton is such a structure (Fig. 4.5), and with careful selection and heat treatment of the steel an enhanced permeability, and therefore improved shielding at low frequencies, has been obtained (Morgan, 1983).

Apart from the use of compression plumbing fittings and copper pipe for double screening, a number of specialized components and systems are available to implement local shielding. These include zipped cable braid shields, electromagnetically shielded plug and socket shells for multiway cables, and adhesive-backed metal foils.

Homemade shielded enclosures can be made from frames of 50×50-mm timber which bolt together to give two boxes, one within the other and separated all round by 15 mm. The inside of the inner and the outside of the outer are covered with sheets of 1-mm aluminium sheet, or 5-mm hole-expanded mesh. The sheets are folded round the edges of the frames (Fig. 4.6) so that a good contact is made when the frames are bolted together. Sheets are joined by butting together over a 50×50-mm frame member, running a 50-mm-wide aluminium strip over the join and securely nailing them at 75-mm intervals with galvanized roofing felt nails (Fig. 4.6). Adjacent sliding doors are provided in each box, using brass angles or channels. The boxes must be insulated from each other, except for a common access panel about 400 mm square. Tongue-and-grooved floor boards on the inner floor support equipment. With care, especially with the doors, an attenuation level of 80 dB has been achieved over the RF range. This construction is very suitable for a dry experimental laboratory, but long-term corrosion of the joints should not be forgotten.

The cutoff waveguide previously referred to consists of a length of metal tube of circular, square or hexagonal cross-section, and of length at least five times the diameter. Seen as a waveguide, a tube will propagate only

Fig. 4.5 — Shielded room facility (courtesy of British Aerospace Dynamics).

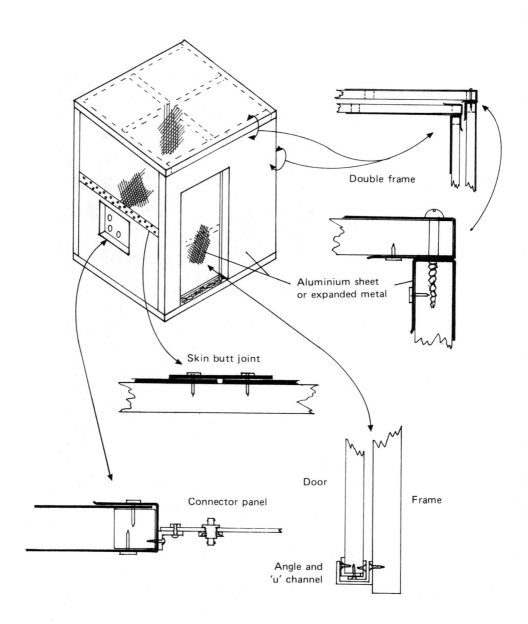

Double frame

Aluminium sheet
or expanded metal

Skin butt joint

Connector panel

Door

Frame

Angle and
'u' channel

electromagnetic waves of frequency higher than the cutoff frequency (Slater
and Frank, 1947; Lee, 1986), where the cutoff frequency f is given by

$$2\ af = c$$

where *a* approximates the tube diameter, but more rigorously depends on the cross-sectional shape. Below the cutoff frequency, propagation drops drastically, and for a 10-mm tube 50 mm long attenuation approaches 100 dB in the region of 10 GHz and remains at this level through the RF spectrum. An array of tubes has the same properties, provided they are electrically bonded together and the edge of the array is bonded to the wall of the enclosure. Metal honeycomb (Fig. 4.7) can be manufactured in large areas and is

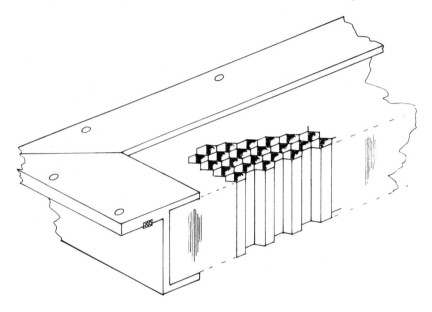

Fig. 4.7 — Honeycomb shield.

frequently used in screened enclosures to admit light and allow ventilation. Fibre optics and other opto-couplers can pass through the honeycomb, as well as plastic pipes, but naturally no metallic leads may pass through.

4.7 DIAGNOSTICS, SHIELDING, AND THE TREE CONFIGURATION

We will attempt to bring together a number of the methods of interference reduction by considering the operation and diagnostics of a typical pulsed-power system of the type considered in Chapter 2. Before the details are considered, it is important first to consider the system configuration in a formal way. Great emphasis has been placed on the relative impedances of the various parts of the system, particularly the less obvious strays.

A complex diagnostic system or a control system can be devised and drawn out in a sequential and logical form which shows all the electrical interconnections. Given the need to avoid multiple ground loops and to minimize the number of cross-connections to reduce interference, it may be asked what the best form of electrical system layout is. Topologically it should be apparent that a radial, or branching, tree-shaped system best satisfies this requirement (Baker *et al.*, 1970; Ricketts *et al.*, 1976). Fig. 4.8,

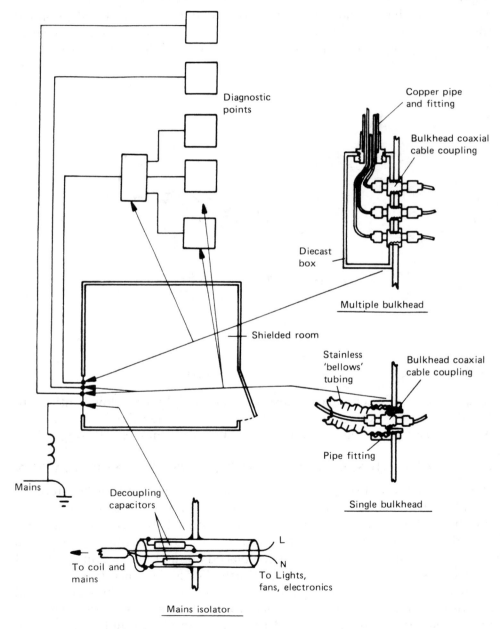

Fig. 4.8 — Multiple diaagnostic leads to a shielded room.

taken from a report by the author (Thornton, 1979), illustrates this arrangement. The shielded diagnostic room containing the recorders forms the trunk, with leads branching out, and in some cases sub-dividing to the diagnostic points. The value of this configuration is as an important basic form which is interference-free. In practice there willl be many cross-connections in the configuration, both actual leads and strays, but if the underlying tree configuration is recognized, the cross-connections can be more easily identified and eliminated, the effects reduced or allowance made. The figure also illustrates bulkhead couplings and methods of double screening, together with a simple mains filter.

Though a means of implementing double screening of leads is shown above, it does not mean that it will be necessary in all cases, However, with the exception of the mains filter, it illustrates the standards and attention to external leads necessary to fully utilize the attenuation capability and to justify the cost of a good quality screened room. Once the need for high sensitivity diagnostics in real time, is recognized, the techniques we have discussed can be implemented. In many cases, there will be a clear need to implement double-screening techniques when using low-signal-level transducers. Although not so immediately apparent, reduction of possible ground loops may also be necessary in the diagnostics.

The above references relate to recommendations for configurations based on experience in electronics, and particularly in communications. Experience with high power, single-pulse systems, and more recently with digital systems, has confirmed these guidelines, which our treatment closely relates to the control of ground loops. In the radial or tree arrangement (Fig. 4.8), each diagnostic point has a separately identifiable lead back to be the recording point, and although some points may have parallel leads, there are no common loops. In the case of the two separate diagnostic radial arms in the figure, the common connection point of their shields is the single panel on the side of the screened room. The common point on the triple arm is the three-way connection box remote from the room. It is particularly important that the outer shield from this box have an electrical integrity comparable with that of the room; it may, for instance be of copper pipe, with soldered or tight compression fittings, or metal bellows tubing may be used.

If a screened room is not itself in direct contact with the ground or building structure, though the main discharge circuit is, it may be possible to connect one or more diagnostic points to the main circuit without creating serious ground loops. The mains ground lead still provides a mains ground, even though the lead is coiled into an inductance, the safety implications of which will be discussed in Chapter 8. In implementing a diagnostic recording system it is worthwhile ensuring that none of the diagnostic leads come into metallic contact with other system leads or metallic pipes. This can be facilitated by the use of plastic support brackets, by threading cables through plastic plumbing or drain pipes, or by laying them in plastic guttering.

In many diagnostic systems there is scope for the use of optical isolation in signal leads, and signals may be piped directly into the screened room through a waveguide isolator.

To illustrate a complete system we have taken the pulse generator of Fig. 2.3 (Chapter 2) and added further diagnostics (Fig. 4.9).

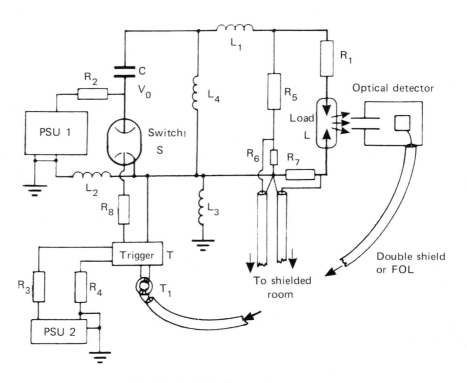

Fig. 4.9 — Multiple diagnostic system.

We have assumed that the load L is some form of gas discharge device, perhaps a laser, or laser pump of negligible inductance, and effective resistance $R_1 = 1\ \Omega$, and that the diagnostics include a voltage divider and a current shunt. The coaxial monitor leads to these latter are assumed to be connected to the nominally grounded side of the discharge circuit. The third diagnostic device is a photodiode measuring the light pulse from the discharge. The pulse generator capacitor C is switched by spark gap S, itself triggered by a high voltage pulse from subsidiary generator T. If C is a 5-μF capacitor, charged to 20 kV, and L_1, R_1 respectively 10 µH and 1 Ω, the discharge waveform will be a damped sinusoid of approximate period 40 µs and peak current 10 kA.

Current is measured by shunt resistor $R_7 \simeq 10$ mΩ, and load potential by a 200:1 divider, $R_5 = 5000$ Ω, $R_6 = 50$ Ω, feeding into 50-Ω coaxial cable. Capacitor C is charged by PSU 1, and associated ground loop connections have been broken by R_2, typically 1000 Ω, and L_2, 100 µH, L_2 provides a secure DC ground for the charging current, and L_4, 100 µH, provides a DC charging path to C across the initially o/c load, L_4 must provide a negligible impedance short circuit across L_1 and the load. If PSU 1 is a high power switched mode supply, the values of R_2, L_2, and L_4 must be compatible with correct operation. L_3, 100 µH, provides a safety DC ground to the building grounding system, but reduces pulse currents to the structure.

Switching of the main spark gap S is by a 20–30 kV trigger pulse of 100 ns or shorter risetime. The trigger pulse is generated using a semiconductor-driven pulse transformer, self-contained within the shielded box T, which interfaces with TTL-level drive pulses (5 V), with 50 Ω input impedance. Thus unit requires low powers, and is supplied from PSU 2, with pulse isolating resistors R_3 and R_4, typically 1000 Ω. The trigger unit is potentially a prolific source of interference in the 10–100-MHz range, and as such it should be completely enclosed, with a short length of coaxial cable (100 mm) connecting the output to the trigger pin, and enclosing limiting resistor R_8. R_8, 50–1000 Ω, limits the trigger current, damps oscillations causing interference, and prevents damage to the semiconductors from return transients when spark gap S fires. To preserve ground-loop isolation, the 5-V drive pulse to T is coupled through a 1:1 pulse transformer T_1 with windings on opposite sides of a small ferrite toroid to give a low stray capacitance.

The system described requires connection to the screened room, and we will assume that the room is several metres from the pulse generator so that the photodiode cannot be shielded in the room, but must be in a well-shielded box near the load. It is likely that the latter would require a self-contained amplifier and battery (Fig. 4.9), with the light entering through a small cutoff waveguide. Since the output signal from the amplifier will be of about 1 V amplitide, double screening of the coaxial cable is used, or alternatively a fibre-optic link could be fitted. As the voltage and current monitor signals are of 100 V, these two coaxial cables are not double screened, Figs 4.3 and 4.8 show how monitor leads may be connected to the screened room. As an alternative to double screening, semi-rigid coaxial cable with a solid copper outer can be used.

Monitoring recorders and the low voltage primary trigger generator are contained within the shielded room. The 100-V monitor signals will require attenuation to about 1 V on entry to the room. The low voltage trigger coaxial cable to the pulse transformer will not normally require double screening since this pulse preceeds any interference, but the possibility of later interference causing damage or double triggering should be considered.

In this example the voltage and current monitors have a common ground, and should not introduce a common mode signal. If they do not have an effective common ground, they can be isolated by coiling each coaxial cable on a large ferrite toroid to reduce the common mode current. For demonstration, more interference techniques have been illustrated than are likely to be required with diagnostic signals as high as 100 V, but this should not be an excuse for ignoring them in practice, as it is usually much more cost-effective in this field to overkill with the easier techniques.

Attaching all metallic leads to the screened room at the single bulkhead panel (Fig. 4.8), reduces the effects of circulating currents at the room. The main leads must pass through this bulkhead, and high quality wideband filters are available to prevent the passage of interference. Though pulses travelling along the mains leads cannot pass through the filter, a ground-loop current along this lead will be transferred to the room skin. Currents as high as those indicated in earlier chapters are undesirable, even in the skin, hence the introduction of the coiled mains lead in Fig. 4.8 which we have previously described. When used in typical pulsed-power systems where the frequency range is restricted to 100 kHz–100 MHz, the inductive mains lead can be used with the simple and cheap single-stage mains filter passing through a waveguide filter (Fig. 4.8), again pioneeered by J. C. Martin and his colleagues at AWE. The decoupling capacitors, 100 nF, must be AC mains rated, and protected by fuses.

Having considered shielding techniques in some detail, it is worth remembering that it is possible to dispense with a shielded room even when working with pulses of 100 kV. But to do so all components carrying this potential must be totally enclosed in small metal boxes or within the coaxial cables, and all circuit and ground loops must be decoupled. The pulse generator described by Seddon and Thornton (1988a) was operated in this way and diagnosed using an oscilloscope in the open laboratory. This implies a shielding ratio between source and diagnostic recorder of 100 dB, and should demonstrate the possibility, by adding a 100-dB screened room, of achieving overall shielding of 200 dB in practice.

REFERENCES

Baker, D., Fleckenstein, W. O., Koehler, D. C., Roden, C. E., & Sabia, R. (1970) *Physical design of electronic systems, Vol. 1, Design technology*, Prentice Hall.

Gagnon, W. L. (1975) *Glass laser power conditioning — 1975*, Lawrence Livermore Laboratory Technology Transfer Series.

Gilmartin, T. J., Godwin, R. O., Davis, J. W., Hagen, W. F.,, Hurley, C. H., Leppelmeier, G. W., Linford, G. J., Myall, J. D., O'Neill, W. C., & Trenholm, J. B. (1975) 10 Kilojoule SHIVA laser system for fusion experiments at LLL. *IEEE/OSA Conference on Laser Engineering and Applications, Washington DC, May 1975*.

Lee, K. H. S. (1986) *EMP interaction: principles, techniques and interaction data*, Hemisphere Publishing Corporation.

Morgan, D. (1983) *An introduction to electromagnetic compatibility*, IEE Summer School Lectures, University of Canterbury, 1983.

Ricketts, L. W., Bridges, J. E., & Miletta, J. (1976) *EMP radiation and protection techniques*, Wiley Interscience.

Seddon, N. & Thornton, E. (1988a) A high voltage, short risetime pulse generator based on a ferrite pulse sharpener. *Rev. Sci. Inst.* **59** (11), 2497.

Seddon, N. & Thornton, E. (1988b) Induction acceleration of projectiles to hypervelocity, *1st European Symposium on Electromagnetic Launch Technology, Delft, Holland, Sept. 1988*.

Slater, J. C. & Frank, N. H. (1947) *Electromagnetism*, McGraw-Hill.

Tesche, F. M. (1978) Topological concepts for internal EMP interaction. *IEEE Transactions on Antennas and Propagation.* **AP26** 60–64.

Thornton, E. (1979) Electrical Interference in Pulsed Power Technology. *Proc. IEE*, **126** (5), 426.

Zepler, E. E. (1945) *The technique of radio design*. Chapman & Hall.

5

Techniques at very high frequencies and at low frequencies

5.1 VERY HIGH FREQUENCIES

In previous chapters we considered interference effects at high frequencies (greater than 1 MHz), where the effects of circuit stray capacitances and inductances cannot be ignored. At still higher frequencies the free-space wavelength becomes comparable with the dimensions of the electrical system itself. In a typical laboratory system this occurs at about 100 MHz, where the wavelength is 3 m and the associated risetime 3–5 ns. What this means is that the time a signal takes to cross the electrical system can no longer be assumed zero; in this case it is 10 ns for 3 m. In practical terms it means that a signal can influence one part of the system at an earlier time than another part. Technically it means that the system has changed from one of lumped electrial parameters to one dominated, on the overall scale, by transit-time and impedance effects.

Two parallel conductors whose spacing is less than $\lambda/5$, can be considered as a transmission line, of which the best known are the coaxial cable and parallel wires.

The impedance of such a line is:

$$Z = (L/C)^{1/2}$$

and the electrical pulse velocity is:

$$v = c/\varepsilon^{1/2} \simeq 200 \, \text{mm/ns for polyethylene dielectric.}$$

L and C are respectively the inductance and capacitance per unit length and ε the dielectric constant in the line. Formulae for L and C are given in Chapter 1 for a number of common configurations, and the reader is left to demonstrate that for wide range of shapes and dimensions the impedance varies over a relatively narrow range, namely 20–300$\rangle$ Ω. Impedances less than 20 Ω require leads spaced by only a fraction of their width, while high impedances require fine wires with large spacings. The propagation velocity of all air-filled parallel shapes is the velocity of light, c, or $0.67c$ when filled with polyethylene as in many coaxial cables. Special transmission lines can be made using materials of high dielectric constant or permeability, or the centre wire can be coiled to give abnormally high or low impedances or low propagation velocities. Transmission lines filled with water, which are used in some very high power pulse generators have impedances of only a few ohms, and a propagation velocity of $c/8$ owing to the high dielectric constant of water (about 70).

The important features of distributed parameter systems are their small range of, and relatively low, impedances, and constant propagation velocity. A convenient figure to remember for the latter is 1 ns/300 mm (12″) in air, or 200 mm with polyethylene core. A system of 1-m dimensions is therefore dominated by transit-time effects for pulses of 1 ns or shorter duration, and by lumped-circuit behaviour for 10 ns or longer pulses. It is not therefore surprising that 1–10 ns is the most difficult time range to analyse in typical laboratory-sized systems, one where many conventional diagnostic devices are at their time response limits. Formal treatments are well known for the faster and slower timescales, but this region is particularly challenging as one of overlap.

It must be realized that the timescales and dimensions can be scaled, and transit-time effects in a large pulsed-power installation of 100-m dimension would start at about 3 MHz frequency, while in semiconductor systems (hybrids or integated circuits) of 10 mm or less dimension 30 GHz is the corresponding frequency. A more exact relation between the size of a system, or component and the electromagnetic frequency where transient-time effects must be considered is important. The common relation of frequency and wavelength is adequate to indicate the transition region, but in the author's experience is often over-optimistically used as a criterion where lumped-parameter theory still accurately applies.

Consider a passive system (Fig. 5.1) consisting of a length l of transmission line of impedance Z_1 inserted in an otherwise matched line of impedance Z_0. A fast risetime square pulse of amplitude V_0 is fed into the system as shown. At the first discontinuity the pulse is partly transmitted and partly reflected, the transmitted amplitude, from elementary textbook theory (e.g. Millman and Taub, 1965), being given by:

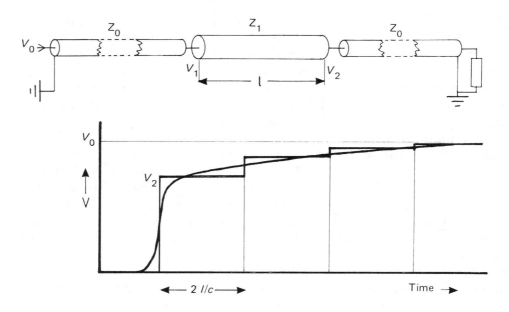

Fig. 5.1 — Mismatched line and transmitted pulse shape.

$$V_1 = 2V_0 Z_1/(Z_0 + Z_1)$$

After a transit distance l, the pulse is again transmitted and reflected at the secondary discontinuity, the transmitted pulse now being:

$$V_2 = 2V_1 Z_0/(Z_0 + Z_1) = 4V_0^2 Z_0 Z_1/(Z_0 + Z_1)^2$$

This transmitted pulse is shown as the first pulse step in Fig. 5.1. The reflected parts of these pulses will suffer further reflections and transmissions at the discontinuities, and the reader may demonstrate that the initial output pulse will be followed by a train of steps of decreasing amplitude, at time intervals of $2l/c$, where c is the line velocity, as shown in Fig. 5.1. The staircase waveform will asymptotically approach the input amplitude V_0.

A most important consideration results from practical mismatch values. For $Z_1 = 2Z_0$, $V_2 = 0.89V_0$ and for $Z_1 = 3Z_0$, $V_2 = 0.75V_0$. For $Z_1 = 0.5Z_0$, and $0.33Z_0$, the results are the same respectively as the two previous values, and so the first step of the pulse is a large fraction of the input amplitude, even for a large mismatch. The pulse may be considered to have effectively reached its peak in three double-transit times. In practice finite input risetimes and ill-defined mismatch points will usually hide step edges, and the pulse is likely to appear as the smoothed waveform in Fig. 5.1. This is a very common shape for fast-risetime pulses. It is not a gaussian shape, and may upset purists by a large 10–90% risetime, which belies the fast front edge. A point of confusion is its similarity to the shape of pulses degraded by transmission through coaxial cables (Taylor and Jackson 1979), and careful analysis may be necessary to separate the two effects.

The conclusion of the foregoing analysis is that the effect of a mismatched section or a discontinuity extends for a time of about five times its actual length. Conversely, transit-time effects must be considered when the electrical length becomes one-fifth of the system dimension. A dielectric-filled component, such as a high impedance probe 200 mm long, has a risetime closer to 5 ns (60 MHz) than to its electrical length of 1 ns. It follows that performance and the detection of faults are facilitated by the use of very small components where possible, and by specifically designing the sub-systems as transmission lines.

When this critical region has been bypassed in the frequency domain by very fast pulses, an interesting situation can occur. Since undesired pulses may enter or be created in a different part of the system from desired pulses, the two may arrive at a diagnostic or other critical point at different times. They may be said to be transit-time-isolated and may not in this sense interfere. Sometimes the two pulses travel by different routes, and one may be inadvertently or intentionally delayed by passing through a coaxial cable.

The concept can be very useful in the control of interference in that it provides an additional dimension to separate interference signals. Transit times can often be accurately estimated, and, if pulse times are measured, the positions of interference sources can be inferred, in a similar way to locating mismatch positions in cables by time-domain reflectometry.

5.2 MICROWAVE FREQUENCIES

The wavelength at a frequency of 10 GHz is 3 cm, and, as discussed in the previous chapter, electromagnetic penetration of small gaps, slots and holes is appreciable. For adequate screening, solid sheets of metal are usually required, and joints must be completely sealed with gaskets of woven wire or conducting elastomers, of which a wide range are available. Even the closely woven braid of coaxial cable must be viewed with suspicion, as well as having attenuation losses. A problem which occurs at high frequencies in shielded enclosures is reflection of an electromagnetic wave from the walls of the enclosure. This can also set up standing waves and constitutes another form of interferance.

Reflections and standing waves can be controlled by the use of absorbers (RAM), and anechoic chambers for use at microwave frequencies are usually lined with wedge-shaped pieces of absorber. To be effective the absorption should occur over a length of several wavelengths, for the imposition of an absorber may introduce additional reflections, hence the use of wedge shapes inside a large shielded enclosure (Fig. 5.2). The use of special microwave-absorbing materials, or stealth, for the structures of military vehicles and aircraft is an extension of this technology to render them non-reflecting to radar pulses.

5.3   TECHNIQUES AT LOW FREQUENCIES

For our purposes a low frequency is defined by the following criteria:

(i) The effects of stray inductance are generally negligible, and EMFs generated by ground-loop currents result primarily from lead resistance only.
(ii) The effects of stray capacitance are negligible.
(iii) The skin effect is generally neglible, so that, in all but very thick conductors, the current flows uniformly through the thickness. Thin metal sheets therefore provide an electrostatic, but not a magnetic, shield. To provide a magnetic shield the material must be of high permeability.

In the laboratory the boundary between low and high frequencies may be taken as the mid-audio range, perhaps 1 kHz, but, depending on the application of the above criteria in specific cases, it could be as high as 100 kHz or as low as 100 Hz. Where very long leads are involved, such as telephone and power lines, 1 kHz may be considered a high frequency. The criterion of relating system dimensions to wavelength, as in the previous chapter, is of some value, because lumped-parameter behaviour applies, except in the special conditions of long power and telephone lines.

It may be tempting to dismiss interference at low frequencies as a simple problem when compared with the effects of circuit strays at high frequencies. However, at high frequencies signal-to-noise ratios 20 dB are often acceptable, even in diagnostic signals, and lower ratios still in trigger and digital circuits. Conversely, in audio hi-fi systems signal-to-noise ratios of 80 dB or higher are necessary, and this is true in other low frequency systems, so the problems can be equally daunting.

Concern with mains hum was a common problem when vacuum valves were used for audio amplification, the hum being introduced through EMFs associated with the heater currents. A similar problem still exists, but the source of EMF is more likely to be power supply smoothing capacitor ripple currents in the ground-loop leads. Reduction of ground-loop resistance is as important as reducing its impedance at high frequencies, though the concept and implementation of a single-point ground is usually easier (Fig. 5.3).

Fig. 5.2 — Microwave absorbers (courtesy of British Aerospace Dynamics).

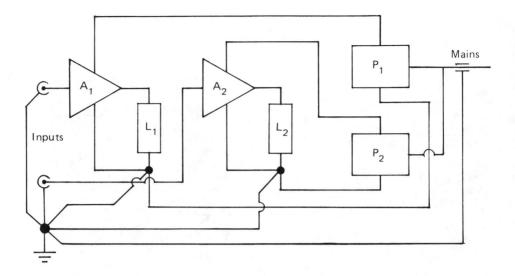

Fig. 5.3 — Single-point ground in low frequency amplifiers.

In amplifiers there is a possibility of feedback and instability from ground loops, and of cross -talk in multiple systems. Fig. 5.3 shows how the use of separate power supplies, P_1 and P_2, combined with a single point ground, for amplifiers A_1 and A_2, and loads L_1 and L_2 reduces the possibility of cross-talk between the circuits, as well as reducing feedback. Short leads and single-point grounding are usually a more cost-effective solutions than massive low resistance conductors. Common mode signals are best reduced in this way as well, but residual low frequency signals can sometimes be balanced out in the inverting and non-inverting inputs of operational amplifiers.

Mains hum can also be introduced by induction pickup from current-carrying leads, and particularly from mains transformers. Use of toroidal transformers, or the use of switched-mode power supplies, which dispense with the mains transformer, are also solutions. However, switched mode power supplies may introduce high frequency interference from the switching transients, which requires reversion to previous chapters! Screening against induction pickup with high permeability magnetic material is less common, though it is sometimes used for cathode ray tubes and for microphone transformers. Coaxial cables can be wound with high permeability tape, and the shielding of screened rooms can be enhanced by the choice of material and wall thickness as in the example in the previous chapter.

Although stray capacitances can generally be ignored at low frequencies, this may not always be so with high input impedance circuits, such as CMOS semiconductors. A stray capacitance of 10 pF at a frequency of 100 Hz has an impedance of approximately $1.5 \times 10^8 \, \Omega$ and could easily transfer a signal to a CMOS input whose input resistance is about $10^{10} \, \Omega$ and capacitance 10 pF.

5.4 TECHNIQUES IN DIAGNOSTIC SYSTEMS

The techniques of interference reduction discussed in the previous chapters are equally applicable to diagnostics, but as diagnostic signals tend to be of low power and signal level, they are more vulnerable to interference. The techniques of shielding, ground-loop isolation and decoupling require careful attention, and have already been discussed in detail. In this section we will consider techniques which are more specific to diagnostic systems and work, not by reducing the interference, but by a sideways step or conversion process.

5.4.1 *Insensitive diagnostics and signal amplification*

In a very limited number of cases it may be possible to amplify a small diagnostic signal close to the diagnostic point for transmission to a remote receiver at higher signal level. This will make the transmitted signal less interference-sensitive. Clearly this a limited technique and can only be effective if the amplifier pickup is significantly less than that of the cable.

A general rule in diagnostic systems is to work with as large signals as can be abstracted from the primary system without significantly perturbing it or degrading the diagnostics. In pulsed-power systems large signals are often available and may be fed to insensitive recorders, with consequent reduction in interference. It is not now a frequently used technique because most commercial diagnostic equipment is of high sensitivity, and well-chosen currently available oscilloscopes and digital recorders are very well screened. Working with large signals can help considerably with interference especially if the signal can thereby be transmitted by coaxial cable to the recorder and attenuated a second time at the recorder. Low sensitivity oscilloscopes were specifically available in the past with direct access to the cathode ray tube 'Y' plates, including the Tektronix 519 (approx. 9 V/div sensitivity), the old AWE Mk iii, iv, and v (30 V/div) series, and the AWE 'T' scope of T. Storr (several kilovolts per division). High recording bandwidths (200 MHz–1 GHZ) were achieved with these systems.

5.4.2 *Optical and frequency conversion*

An electrical signal may be converted to an optical one to avoid interference during transmission, but the techniques of frequency conversion and carrier modulation have long been used to improve signal-to-noise ratios in radio and transmission-line communications. An awareness of these latter techniques is critical in interference control in communications and in remote diagnostics, and the reader is referred to specialized text books on radio communication fundamentals (e.g. Goodyear, 1971; Pierce and Posner, 1980). RF conversion is not generally suited to fast-pulsed signals owing to the high bandwidths involved, and here optical conversion is useful.

Optical signals can conveniently be transmitted large distances by fibre-optic links. Conversion is usually, but not exclusively, performed by light-emitting diodes (LEDs) or lasers in the near-infrared, at wavelengths in the range 8–1.5 μm. Neither is the technique exclusively limited to conversion of voltage signals; electric and magnetic fields can rotate the plane of polarization, and hence vary the transmission of a laser light beam in suitable materials, including optical fibres (Smith, 1980, Osborne and Hutchinson, 1986). This diagnostic method has the advantage of no electrical transmitter of interference.

Simple electro-optic isolators are generally non-linear and are more suited to transmitting pulses. Since, however, they can be made very fast, they are used in digital systems, with analogue bandwidths as high as 1 GHz. As discussed in a previous chapter, the transmitter and receiver units must be very well shielded, for internal signals are small, possibly millivolts in the receiver.

5.4.3   *Low frequency diagnostics*

Real-time diagnostics of fast waveforms is the ideal, but there are many instances where a low frequency or DC measurement can give useful information about performance. Such a measurement can, with reservations, give relative levels of shot-to-shot performance, or average power, or energy outputs. The reservations are that the low frequency diagnostic must not be susceptible to the high frequency interference, and the diagnostic must be calibratable in terms of the primary system performance or, on a relative scale, linearly related to it. A common diagnostic device — so common that it is not always recognized as such — is the power supply voltmeter. In well-characterized pulsed systems it will predetermine the pulse amplitude and can indicate a number of faults and misfires. Meters normally respond only to near-DC, but digital and analogue meters may be damaged by transients and even jeopardize the operator and should be decoupled by filters, a point which will be considered in Chapter 8.

Other slow-time diagnostics include the integrated light output from gas discharges and lasers, X-ray dosimetry from flash X-ray generators and plasmas, infrared emission and calorimetry. The heat output from a wide range of electrical devices is an important diagnostic in the energy conversion process, and is used as an absolute measure of power in RF and microwave systems and in high power pulsed systems, e.g. Perkin *et al.* (1971), Thornton and Harris (1973). The latter reference provides an interesting example of the low susceptibility of slow diagnostics to fast transients. An array of graphite calorimeters absorbed the energy of a 100-kA pulsed electron beam, yet the thermocouple galvanometers, sensitive to DC currents of a microamp, showed no observable transient deflection or damage, and merely recorded the slow rise to temperature equilibrium in the graphite.

Many fast electrical signals still yield useful information if integrated, when the signal can be read in slower time. This can be used as a way of eliminating interference if the desired signal is of single polarity and the interference is oscillatory, for the integral of the latter is zero. Care is necessary, however, when using integrating circuits, for a passively integrated signal is usually much smaller in amplitude than the primary signal. The loss in amplitude must be compensated by a greater reduction in interference susceptibility by the longer timescale. The use of a totally different method of recording the signal may accomplish this.

REFERENCES

Goodyear, C. C. (1971) *Signals and Information*, Butterworth.

Millman, J. & Taub, H. (1965) *Pulse, digital and switiching waveforms*. McGraw Hill.

Osborne, M. R. & Hutchinson, M. H. R. (1986) Electro-optic voltage measurement in a high power excimer laser. *Rev. Sci. Instrum.* **57**(9), 2353.

Perkin, J. L., Morris, E., & Large, D. W. (1971), *J. Phys. D: Appl. Phys.*, **4**, 974.

Pierce, J. R. Pierce, & Posner, E. C. (1980) *Introduction to communication science and systems*, Plenum Press.

Smith, A. M. (1980) Optical fibres for current measurement applications, *Optics and Laser Technology*, **12**(1), 25.

Taylor, T. G., & Jackson, M. C. (1979) *Investigation of the pulse response of 50 Ω cables*, AWE, Aldermaston, SFO Note No. 2/79.

Thornton, E., & Harries, R. R. (1973) Development of a pulsed relativistic electron beam of large diameter and uniform flux, *J. Phys. E.*, **6**, 1223.

6

Microelectronics and interference as an engineering concept

6.1 CONCEPTS OF CHANGE IN SIZE

In this chapter we shall extend the interference concepts established in the previous chapters in systems of laboratory size to the much smaller world of microelectronics. We have tried to consider electrical interference in terms of the fundamental physical operation of components and circuit elements before extending it to systems, and attempted to quantify it in similar terms. Therefore it should be relatively easy to make a step down in size by an order of magnitude (to 100 mm) to consider printed circuits (PCs), and by a further two orders of magnitude (to 1 mm) to consider integrated circuit (IC) chips.

However, when making such steps it is vital to take into account all the necessary scaling factors, and, as there are a number of interacting factors to be considered, the problem may not be straightforward. Firstly it is important to alter the limiting time and frequency criteria already established for lumped and distributed circuit parameters. On a 1-mm-square IC dice the dimensions of components and leads are so small that it should behave according to lumped circuit theory up to a frequency of about 100 GHz. This greatly exceeds the operating frequency of semiconductor devices on the dice. We will be concerned with the stray impedances of micrometre-thick conductors and not with transit time effects on small dice.

The conductors on PCs and ICs are much thinner than their laboratory-sized counterparts. Crudely the resistance varies with thickness, but inductance varies with log thickness, as indicated in earlier chapters. Ground loops are therefore more likely to be resistive, rather than inductive. Unlike most wired systems, PCs and ICs are quasi-two-dimensional, which can have the beneficial effect of reducingt stray capacitances between components. However, the use, of thin, multiple layers can increase the capacitance between adjacent conductors, which can have both good and bad effects on interference transmission. There is a trend towards increasing the number of deposited layers in order to pack more components into a given volume and reduce transit-time effects. This will increase the effect of stray capacitance and will require greater attention to inbuilt shielding layers.

The structure of an IC normally shows a much greater degree of regularity than a wired circuit, is usually much more complicated, and as such may be more suited to computer design and analysis. It is, therefore, perhaps appropriate to introduce in this chapter the idea of interference as an engineering concept.

6.2 PRINTED CIRCUITS

In our discussion, the distinction between a PC and an IC is primarily one of size, and a PC will most likely contain ICs. When discussing a printed circuit, an IC thereon will be considered functionally as a semiconductor of appropriate input and output characteristic performing the same function. Then the sensitivity to an interference signal in the PC board (PCB) at the input of the IC can be assessed in terms of the signal amplitude and the function as an analogue or digital element. The way in which the internal design of the IC may affect its sensitivity to interference will be considered qualitatively in the next section.

The conductors in a PC are usually of smaller cross-section than those in wired circuits. A copper track strip 0.025 mm (0.001″) thick, 0.5 mm wide and 75 mm long, (as in Fig. 6.1) has a resistance of 0.1 Ω. A current of 1 mA in such a lead will produce an EMF of 100 μV, sufficient to affect a high sensitivity operational amplifier input, but not a digital circuit. However, for a pulsed ground-loop current of 10 A, the EMF is 1 V, which is sufficient to switch digital circuitry. The track inductance of the above strip is typically 0.1 μH, and its impedance will be similar in magnitude to the resistance at a frequency of about 1 MHz. Strictly we should consider both resistance and inductance in the effect of the leads, but the main point is that resistance is more important than in normal wiring.

The track resistance can be reduced in design by widening the track, and in operation by a thick layer of solder tinning or by soldering a wire over the track. It is usual to etch away all copper foil except for the narrow conductors, but it can be an advantage to leave all the copper outside the conductors as a low resistance ground plane with lower ground-loop impedance and providing some shielding. PC tracks often follow circuitous routes to avoid crossing,

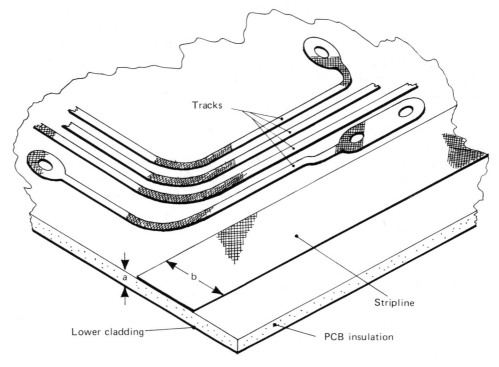

Fig. 6.1 — PCB Track details.

and this simplifies manufacture at the expense of higher track resistance and greater intertrack stray coupling. Double-sided PCBs greatly facilitate track crossing, and much shorter track routes can be achieved by using both sides. In some high frequency applications the second side can be left as a complete screen, with components mounted from this side (normal components) or mounted directly on the track (surface mount).

Opposing tracks on double-sided PCBs can be used to form a transmission line as well as a shield, (Fig. 6.1), which at high frequencies reduces interference pickup as well as providing matching. The impedance of a stripline is given (see Chapter 2) by:

$$Z = 377 \frac{a}{b} \varepsilon^{1/2}$$

where ε is the dielectric constant of the board material.

For $a = 1.6\,mm$, $b \simeq 5.5$ mm for a fibreglass board and 50 Ω stripline.

Although the higher resistance of narrow PC tracks is normally undesirable in interference control, there are instances where it may be beneficial. In a PCB containing a number of ICs whose power supply leads are individually decoupled by separate capacitors, the resistance between each IC along the power tracks assists in decoupling them. It reduces the amplitude of loop currents passing between the ICs via these tracks. It also increases the EMF between them, and the relative effects must be balanced.

The criteria for the design of an electronic circuit which includes PCBs are generally based on sequential positioning of components following the functional diagram. This keeps lead lengths to a minimum and reduces stray inductances and capacitances, thereby reducing uncontrolled feedback and promoting operational stability. It is these same criteria which are most likely to reduce interference pickup.

6.3 INTEGRATED CIRCUITS

The particular way in which an IC is constructed and used makes it possible to consider its interference susceptibility from two viewpoints. Though the circuit on the chip may be extremely complicated, with many components and leads, the chip itself is usually very small and is connected to the outside world by a limited number of fine wires to its pins. Even in a strong electromagnetic field the tiny chip is unlikely itself to pick up a large signal. In the first instance the behaviour towards external interference is more likely to be determined by pickup in the above fine wires and by the functional response of the chip to the interference as an externally injected signal. Clearly the signal amplitudes are critical, particularly in digital circuits.

In the second instance the IC is considered from a different standpoint. If we imagine it greatly magnified (Fig. 6.2), it appears somewhat similar to a dense PCB layout, with high component packing density and (probably) thin leads. Independently of its overall function, and particularly with fast digital transients, internal signals will couple through strays in exactly the same physical ways as discussed in earlier chapters. It will possess ground loops, stray capacitances, and possibly transmission lines like laboratory-sized systems. Interference may therefore be generated internally by the voltage and current pulses from its active components.

Both of these separate views are simplifed, and, if loop currents flow across a chip from an external source, both viewpoints must be considered together and the internal structure examined. Clearly internally generated interference is unlikely to affect common mass-produced ICs which have been carefully functionally tested, but larger-area (large-scale integration) and user-function-programmable chips may have built-in interference.

In an electric field of 10 kV/m the field drop across a 1-mm chip is 10 V overall and is not likely to result in significant pickup, which illustates the statement of the first paragraph in this section. However, with chips of

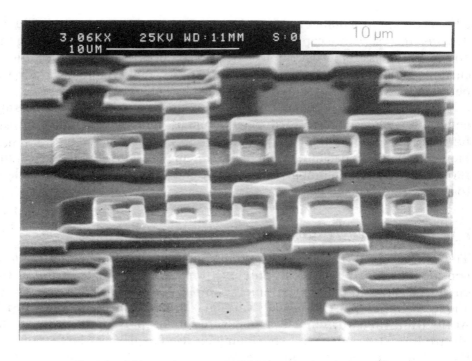

Fig. 6.2 — IC layout (courtesy of GEC Plessey Semiconductors Ltd).

100×100 mm, induced pickup may be much larger, and its effect will be more dependent on decoupling, layout and local shielding. In large-area ICs the problems of increased direct internal interference generation and pickup as the number of leads and components grows, together with increased pickup and transfer from more external leads, could become a nightmare, particularly so if the IC is a computer controlling a complex, expensive and critical system. However, ICs are multilayer devices and are undergoing continual development towards more complex structures. It should therefore be practiable to include in the structure during manufacture local screening and decoupling, and if necessary a breakdown into a cell configuration with individual interference hardening. An interesting and very challenging area.

6.4   INTERFERENCE — AN ENGINEERING CONCEPT

In the previous section it was emphasized that interference in an IC, making appropriate allowances for size and scale, can be treated in a similar way to that in a large pulsed-power installation whose linear dimensions are about five orders of magnitude larger. The ability of a system to pick up or to generate interference is critically dependent on its design as a system, as well as on the detailed design and the quality of manufacture of its parts. In the latter instance, the integrity of shields and the resistaance of contacts can be very important.

Many of the parameters we have considered important in the generation and control of interference are difficult to quantify accurately. There is often a tendency to associate accuracy with importance. Here this could be fatal. Interference is very real, whether it can be estimated to 1% or 50%, and will not go away without positive effort. It is part of the design of the system and is built in alongside the deliberately chosen working functions. Interference should therefore be considered as an engineering concept in complex electrical systems, albeit an undesirable one. As already pointed out, it is usually far easier and more cost-effective to remove interference in the design stages of a system. Fig. 6.3, for which the author is indebted to I. P. MacDiarmid, graphically illustrates this point, and one may expect the cost ordinate to be exponential. Many of the techniques are so simple and cheap that considerable overkill in the design and construction is far more desirable than the tracking down of interference at a later stage. Once it is realized that the production of interference in most systems is as inevitable as it is unintentional when it is designed and built, the way is open to treat it as an engineering concept.

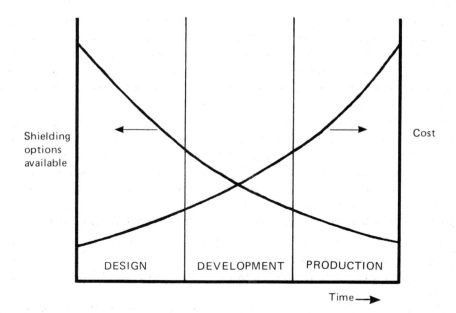

Fig. 6.3 — Interference engineering.

7

Lightning, EMP and other sources

7.1 LIGHTNING

Lightning is the oldest, though now perhaps not the best-known, electrical interference source. It is well known as a source of damage in electrical power transmission systems, telephone systems and in permanent RF transmitters. Damage protection has long been built into these systems, but less concern has been given to interference in the sense in which we have been discussing it in the previous chapters, because a momentary interruption in the service is unimportant. Greater reliance on semiconductors and more critical applications in communications now means that greater attention must be given to the 'electronics' effects of the lightning signal, as well as to gross damage effects. Lightning strikes to aircraft is another area of concern, highlighted by changes from metal skin to non-metallic composites in the construction and by the greatly increased use of semiconductor-based control systems.

The magnitude and time variation of current in a lightning stroke is dependent on the cloud charge distribution, on the polarity, and on whether the stroke is to another cloud or to ground (Schonland, 1953). The common features are currents of tens of kiloamps, charge flows in excess of 10 C, and durations usually in excess of 1 ms (see Fig. 7.1, which is based on Phillpot (1977)). In certain circumstances, currents in excess of 200 kA, rising in 1–2 µs, can occur, and total charge flows exceeding 300 C have been recorded.

The high voltage gradients and high rates of current rise make the strikes a powerful electromagnetic radiation source, though their infrequency has not made this a serious problem. The main concern has been the protection

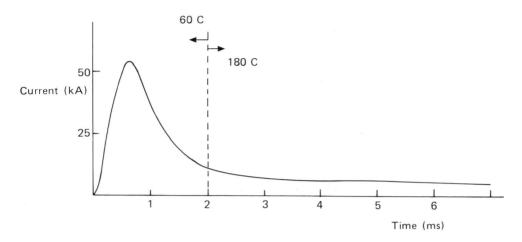

Fig. 7.1 — Typical positive ground flash I.

of permanent installations, such as power and telephone lines, from damage caused by the high energy and charge flow. Included in this category are large or important buildings, wireless masts, and explosives stores. Large aircraft have to date been metal-skinned, and could generally be expected to survive a lightning strike with local damage at the strike point, while the electrical system, excluding antennas, is shielded by the skin. Damage protection of this kind is outside the scope of this book, but recent developments in aircraft design have emphasized electrical interference: firstly, the use of composite materials in the aircraft structure, and secondly, the use of digital control systems.

Protection of a building or other object against lightning by shielding or lightning conductors will, in general, influence the magnitude and path of current flow when lightning strikes the object. The first round of protection required is against structural damage, e.g. melting of aircraft rivets, an aspect outside the scope of this book. However, this protection may influence current paths and therefore the form of induced electromagnetic signals within the object or system. Hence the process of interference generation and corresponding preliminary topological breakdown to study it can follow the following route:

(1) Establishment of the primary current distribution of the lightning pulse over the system.
(2) Coupling of the primary (e.g. skin) current to secondary conductors such as chassis, pipes and cable looms, followed by a further coupling into

critical electrical and electronic sub-systems and components. The aim is to establish current and voltage (field) magnitudes.

(3) Consideration of non-linear effects resulting from the high primary currents and charge flow, such as sparking and internal electrical break-down. This process can also result in re-radiation of energy at higher frequencies.

When the magnitudes, frequency spectra, and signal routes can be identified, they can be treated by the techniques discussed in the previous chapters. Lightning protection in large and critical structures containing vulnerable equipment, such as electronics in aircraft, is both complex and specialized, and dedicated treatments are available (e.g. Golde, 1977; Phillpot, 1977; Burrows, 1981). This last reference illustrates electrical installation techniques to minimize lightning effects, while the second reference points out the importance of realistic simulation. Performing the latter on a large scale requires the use of high energy pulsed-power systems such as those at the Lightning Test and Technology Facility at the UK Culham Laboratory.

The use of composite materials, including graphite fibres, is a field currently undergoing rapid development. It is perhaps most obvious in the aircraft industry, but is far more wide ranging and includes other forms of structures, e.g. ships. Many composites are insulating, or in the case of graphite fibres only partly conducting, and the absence of an outer metal shell may leave the enclosed structure vulnerable to EMPs. As such it may require special screening or testing and be a suitable candidate for the use of non-electric actuators and controls or the use of fibre-optic links. Graphite fibre is particularly interesting, since the conducting fibres are usually bounded by an insulator, and a large component may produce extensive sparking during a lightning strike, even at points remote from the strike site.

In power transmission systems, unlike most of the techniques for interference reduction discussed in previous chapters, diversion of lightning and other surges by flashover, or by breakdown in a controlled place or element, is an important means of dissipating the surge energy and preventing damage. As a technique for the protection of a vast amount of low power equipment against mains surges from both remote lightning strike and from a wide range of manmade causes, it is a rapid growth area. It is therefore appropriate to consider interference reduction from surges by this technique in this chapter.

The diversion of a lightning strike or other power surge implies the passage of a high current into a circuit, with or without the use of an ancillary energy dumping element. This is a clear example of a ground-loop current and in previous chapters we have taken great trouble to stress how undesirable this is as a source of interference, in many cases advocating increasing the ground-loop impedance to reduce the current. This is an anomaly which we will attempt to resolve.

The surge from a remote source may be controlled locally in two basic

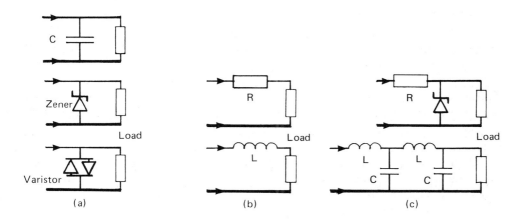

Fig. 7.2 — Suppressors: (a) shunt, (b) series, (c) composite.

ways (Fig. 7.2). Either it can be presented with a temporary short circuit in its path (a) or an open circuit (b). Either will inhibit the passage of the surge further down the line, but each method has different consequences. The series suppressor is the technique which we have considered of great importance in the reduction of ground-loop currents in transient interference. However, if a high power surge is presented with an open circuit, the circuit inductance will result in the generation of a large EMF, which is likely to result in flashover and diversion of energy into undesirable places. For high power surges, such as lightning, a shunt device may be the only practicable technique whereby the large energy can be dissipated in the power lines themselves or in the shunt device. The concern is then that the ground-loop current will introduce additional electromagnetic interference. A partial solution to this latter problem is a composite device (Fig. 7.2(c)), which is the basis of a wide range of commercial devices, most of which are used to suppress mains transients to sensitive equipment such as computers.

It should be noted that the suppressors which are purely capacitive and inductive absorb no energy, while semiconductor and resistive devices do, and the consequences to the circuit of the absorbed energy must be considered. The shunt device must be capable of safely absorbing the maximum energy, otherwise it becomes a liability during or after the first pulse. Mains suppressors for high performance shielded rooms are multistage devices within their own screened box (Fig. 7.3) and have suppressors in each mains conductor. An important point to remember when dealing with transient interference is that few devices break the ground loop between the mains and the protected device, and a large ground-loop current may still flow.

A wide range of specialist and other devices are available as shunt suppressors, under various trade names. Simple capacitors will serve in many instances, though in the mains should have adequate AC voltage and surge current rating. Voltage-dependent resistors (VDRs), sealed spark gaps, and high power zener diodes are freely available over a wide range of ratings. Zeners can operate in less than 5 ns, spark gaps and VDRs of large size can cope with the full current of a lightning strike, and a small VDR can absorb 1 kJ of energy at 5 kA, while passing less than 1 mA of current at operating voltage.

Ordinary diodes and zeners singly and in combination are cheap and effective suppressors at low energies whilst the author has made small spark gap suppressors to bypass sensitive connectors and cables by soldering two stiff, sharp-ended copper wires to tags so that the ends form a 0.5 mm gap. This will break down on a transient of a few kilovolts.

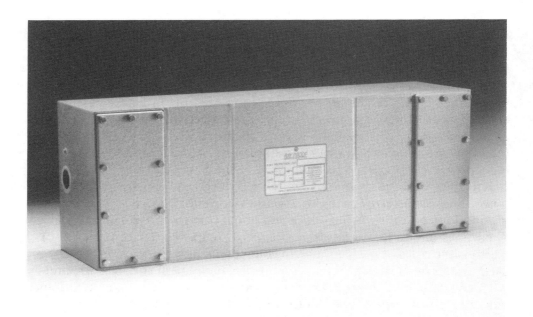

Fig. 7.3 — High performance mains suppressor (courtesy of Ray Proof Ltd).

7.2   NUCLEAR AND ALLIED EMP

Lightning and radio interference protection have been implemented for a long time, but the current concern with transient interference, and many protection techniques, can be directly traced back to the large EMP first observed in nuclear weapon bursts after the Second World War. At an early stage in testing, extensive shielding of the electrical diagnostics was found to be essential, and unclassified information on the EMP later became available (Kompaneets, 1959, Glasstone, 1962). During the 1950s there was a growth in pulsed-power technology as a result of nuclear fusion research and in the 1960s as a further result of weapon simulation, and it is from experimental work in these areas that much of the basic interference technology discussed in the previous chapters was developed. Concern about the effects of EMPs on military systems has furthered shielding developments and resulted in the availability of a wide range of shielding hardware which is rapidly entering the civil field.

The nuclear EMP results from the large separation associated with high

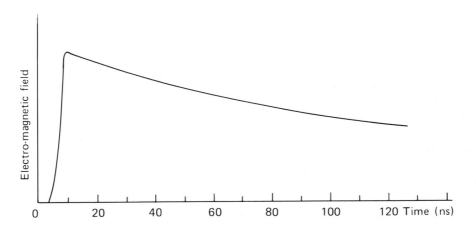

Fig. 7.4 — Representative EMP.

energy charged particles and ionizing radiation (Longmire, 1978; Lee, 1986). The radiated EMP shape and amplitude is dependent on the weapon and its burst altitude, but from the references a representative pulse is inferred (Fig. 7.4) with a 5-ns risetime and a decay time of several hundred nanoseconds. In the atmosphere, however, the ionization may persist for long periods, the pulse tail extends well beyond the timescale of Fig. 7.4, and the frequency spectrum extends from virtually DC to the 100-MHz region. The essential difference between this pulse and those discussed in earlier chapters is in the lower frequency components, and as such it can be considered as a stringent standard for shielding. Shielding against a nuclear EMP has resulted in the design of simulators to generate the pulse by purely electric or electronic means, some such pulsers being of considerable size.

7.3 SIMULATORS

Shielding or, to use the more military term, electromagnetic hardening, of electronic systems is likely to require practical checking, since to use the actual interference source is not practicable. Therefore some form of simulation is necessary. Excluding constant-wave sources, high power pulse generators can often provide realistic interference power levels, and fast-rising pulses provide a wide frequency spectrum. A few large installations are available to irradiate complete systems, such as aircraft and military vehicles (Fig. 7.5).

Interference signals from small, low power simulators can be injected directly into a localized part of the system, for example a cable loom, and realistically simulate the effects with smaller equipment. Alternatively, small components can be mounted inside a parallel-plate transmission line to subject them to a high field (Fig. 7.6). Ensuring that the simulation is realistic is usually a challenge.

Extensive use of digital electronics has ensured that this technology has spread to civil applications. Much simulation and test is performed with conventional constant-wave RF and microwave sources, but the low available powers are often a serious handicap. Pulsed sources of three and more orders of magnitude greater output power can often be obtained or constructed for a modest outlay using pulsed-power technology.

The devices used in simulator pulse generation cover a wide range, from multimegavolt Marx generators, through types of switched transmission lines, to transistor switches of a few volts. It is an inevitable irony that some of the best-hardened systems are the diagnostics used to test and calibrate simulators. The parallel-plate transmission line (Fig. 7.5), with matched, tapered ends, is commonly used to test components or systems mounted within it, is driven from one end by the pulse generator, and can be made very large by making the plates of closely spaced wires. It provides a relatively uniform field over a large area and a constant impedance. Specified EMP test electric fields may be as high as 100 kV/m, though it is of interest to point out that fields within critical parts of the simulator pulse generator may be two orders of magnitude higher. Most EMP simulators have microsecond pulse duration, corresponding to the main frequency components in a nuclear EMP, but lightning, as discussed earlier, requires millisecond pulses. The pulses generated by a wide range of trigger and switching transients, together

Fig. 7.5 — Irradiation facility (courtesy of British Aerospace Military Aircraft).

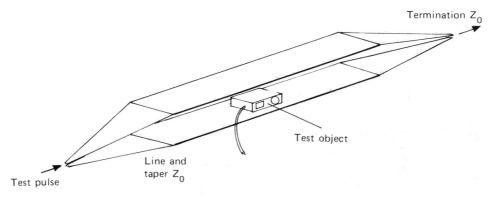

Fig. 7.6 — Parallel line simulator.

with electrical flashover, usually have associated risetimes of a few nanoseconds, and durations from nanoseconds to microseconds, of which a nuclear EMP shape is representative.

7.4   INDUSTRIAL AND DOMESTIC EMP

The electrical supply system is subject to a wide range of surges caused by lightning, load changes, switch transients and faults. An increase in the use of digital systems and of switched-mode power supplies has introduced faster transients into the system and extended concern beyond traditional damage prevention and safety hazards towards data corruption and system malfunction. EMP has been introduced into this area, and the transients which occur in all industrial and domestic electrical systems must be considered in the light of the electromagnetic interference they generate.

The systems and equipment which are most likely to be vulnerable are those discussed in previous chapters and those which are digitally controlled, e.g. electronically controlled industrial processing, domestic appliances, computers, telephones, and other communication systems. In particular, interconnected systems with long communication links are likely to be particularly vulnerable. The latter types of system can be expected to be limited in their speed of response, since necessary interference reduction techniques are likely to include considerable redundancy in the form of duplicated channels, repetition of critical signals, coding, and correlation techniques. Use of fibre-optic links is one way to offset these problems, since they offer increased bandwidth as well as greater interference immunity.

1992 European Community interference standards require the control of electromagnetic emissions from all electrical devices, including humble domestic ones, and this is causing a considerable increase in EMP awareness.

The physical processes which cause interference transcend civil, military and appliance barriers, and it is convenient to consider analogies with pulsed-power systems. The switched discharge involving inductors and capacitors considered in our basic approach in Chapter 1 is a useful starting point for systems such as automobile ignition and domestic thermostats. Techniques for reducing the effects of EMP, such as critical damping of circuits, transient diversion and screening, have already been discussed.

From a practical viewpoint the transfer of electrical interference through the mains and the effects of pickup by the mains can be considerably reduced by the following simple techniques:

(1) Use of mains filters at equipment interfaces of the type discussed in section 7.1. Simple filters attenuate a wide range of transients in the range 1 kHz–100 MHz.

(2) The transient suppressors also previously discussed have wide application, and can suppress increases in voltage in critical DC lines. Care must be taken to ensure that the associated current surge does not result in further EMP generation.

(3) Decoupling of equipment from its main power supply or internal decoupling of power lines is practicable in many cases of modern electronic equipment operating on low powers. DC lines can be decoupled with passive series impedance, batteries can be used to provide isolated power, large PSU smoothing capacitors work similarly, and a wide range of DC–DC isolated power supplies are available.

(4) It is quite practicable to introduce fast sensor circuits to detect power supply transients and actuate isolators which temporarily decouple the PSU; this is an active form of the passive decoupling of (3). It is easy to include a wide variety of these techniques in a system, but they should not be used as a substitute for investigating the interference source and transfer mechanism.

REFERENCES

Burrows, B. J. C. (1981) *Designers guide to the installation of electrical wiring and equipment in aircraft to minimise lightning effects*. UKAEA Culham Laboratory Report CLM-R212, HMSO.

Glasstone, S. (Ed.) (1962) *The effects of nuclear weapons*, US Govt. Printing Office.

Golde, R. H. (1977) *Lightning Protection Vols* 1 & 2. Academic Press.

Kompaneets, A. S. (1959) Radio emission from an atomic explosion, *Soviet Physics JETP* (English Translation) **35** (8), 1076.

Lee, K. S. H., (Ed.) (1986) *EMP interaction*: *principles, techniques and reference data*, Hemisphere.

Longmire, C. L. (1978). On the electromagnetic pulse produced by nuclear explosions. *IEEE Trans. on Antennas and Propagation* **AP26** (1), 3.

Phillpot, J. (1977) *Recommended practice for lightning simulation and techniques for aircraft*, UKAEA Culham Laboratory Report CLM-R163, HMSO.

Schonland, B. F. J. (1953) *Atmospheric electricity*, 2nd Edition, Methuen.

8

The effects of interference and ground loops on control systems and electrical safety

8.1 ELECTRIC SHOCK HAZARDS

As a particular approach to the problem of electrical interference, the treatment in this book and the methods of quantifying signals are primarily based on laboratory pulsed-power systems and on their associated diagnostics. It is hoped that it has been shown that these systems are so wide-ranging that the techniques illustrated are also widely applicable in other areas. The larger laboratory installations are also particularly useful in illustrating the important human interface with the system. The system is usually controlled through a hard-wired, or microprocessor-based logical, sequential-firing procedure. This should be designed to operate the system correctly, while preventing hazard, including electric shock to the operator and to other visitors. It must also be failsafe against operator error and absent-mindedness.

Serious shock hazards from high voltage DC components such as charged capacitors and power supplies are well-understood and are prevented by enclosures, interlocked through the control system as considered in the next section. They are also prevented by the correct use of energy dumps, an important subject but outside the scope of this treatment. The electric shock hazards considered in this section are transient EMFS created during operation in conductors and metallic components which are nomimally grounded; these may hazard not only the operator, but even personnel some distance away. That these hazards are real can be illustrated by an early experience of the author. A high voltage capacitor was being tested by repetitive discharging inside an enclosure, and an irate colleague from the far end of the corridor, not from next door, informed us that a spark was jumping from his telephone to the radiator alongside, in synchronism with the sound crack of the discharge.

Clearly transient EMFS of this kind can be considered as another form of interference, with a person as the receiver. Any person in contact with a metal part of the system, such as control or diagnostic equipment, is at risk of a transient electric shock. This type of hazard is very difficult to quantify, and it is likely that shocks involving currents and voltages which would be serious at DC are quite frequent, but unfelt, in impulses. Qualitatively the author can confirm this, and J. C. Martin at AWE Aldermaston pointed out many years ago that the inner, moist layers of the skin may form a conducting, screened enclosure for the body at pulse frequencies. It should be pointed out that these comments apply only to fast, single pulses, whose magnitude and duration is unsufficient to produce any heating effects or nerve response. They do not apply to continuously applied fields of any frequency, for which rigorous safety standards exist.

In Chapter 2, the importance of ground loops in generating and propagating interference signals was considered in detail, and it was demonstrated how large EMFS can be generated across leads normally considered to be at ground potential. There is, therefore, the risk of electric shock, and the common and useful idea of keeping one hand in a pocket may be insufficient if the human circuit is completed by a stray capacitance.

Grounding is normal safety practice, but ground loops can actually increase EMFS if their presence results in large ground-loop currents. However, all ground potential conductors should be grounded; it is not only a common legal requirement, but an obvious protection against mains and power supply hazards, some of which will exist in inoperative periods, such as during servicing. These apparently opposing requirements can be partly resolved by reducing the number of grounding points, but it may be helpful to state the aim of safety in this way:

'The aim of electrical safety is to prevent the existence of hazardous electrical gradients between parts of the human body.'

Grounding is one way of achieving this at DC and mains frequencies. Under pulse conditions, however, multiple grounding may actually increase the hazard, and it is also necessary to reduce loop currents, which can be achieved by breaking ground loops. Provided the ground loop is continuous at low frequencies and broken at high frequencies, for instance by an inductance, both conditions can be satisfied. It is an obvious additional requirement to exclude personnel from the position of the loop break during operation, since high EMFS may be developed across it. The safety officer, who by default may also be the designer, is therefore responsible for the identification and control of ground loops. Reduction of ground-loop currents in the control room and other access areas gives greater confidence to personnel that metal enclosures and barriers here provide a good approximation to a Faraday enclosure.

A particular area of hazard concerns the monitoring leads from a system to the control or diagnostic recording rooms. As these leads are often connected directly into the heart of the high power system, they can bring interference straight to the operator, in addition to faulting the electrical systems. One simple example, the monitoring of the DC charging potential in a high voltage pulsed system, illustrates this point, the writer being aware of a case in which a fault resulted in the control room meter exploding. Though this is rare, there are more frequent examples where the energy in the interference pulse is sufficient to damage analogue or digital meters.

Consider a typical voltage monitor circuit which would usually consist only of the resistors R_1 and R_2, together with meter M (Fig. 8.1), R_1, typically

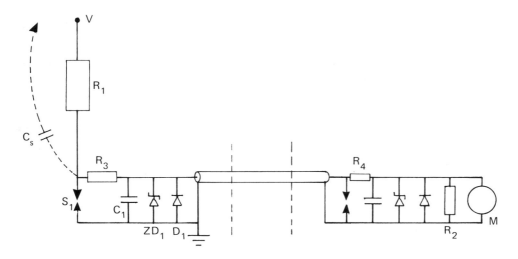

Fig. 8.1 — Decoupling of monitor circuit.

100 MΩ, is the high voltage section of the divider, and M with R_2 forms the low voltage calibrating section. In the presence of high voltage transients, a small stray capacitance C can transfer sufficient energy to damage a meter; a

flashover across R_1 can do much worse. A high degree of protection can be easily provided by the addition of the additional components shown in Fig. 8.1. R_3 and C_1 provide decoupling against transients, and typically they are 10 kΩ and 100 nF in value respectively. ZD_1 is a zener diode of about 10 V rating to protect C_1 and the low voltage leads should the meter of R_2 become detached or open-circuit. D_1 likewise protects against reverse DC, while S_1, a spark gap made with two stiff wires soldered with ends facing and 0.5 mm apart, forms a cheap last-ditch suppressor. A coaxial lead is coupled to the remote meter, and here the figure shows that the same components are repeated. This arrangement may seem like a large overkill, but it provides a wide range of protection, it is easy to make, and, apart from the meter, uses very cheap and easily obtained components. Unless S_1 breaks down, it produces no ground-loop currents, and the system provides about 80 dB of voltage attenuation for a microsecond transient.

The example considered is one in which steps have been taken to protect personnel, but as the meter has also been protected from transient and slower interference, and as it is part of the control system, it makes a convenient introduction to the next section.

8.2   CONTROL SYSTEMS

The control system of a large or small installation performs a sequence of logical operations which are designed to ensure that each part of the system works correctly in magnitude and time, including safety functions. In complex systems it is obvious that a large degree of monitoring and feedback will be necessary. The logical functional system design can be very challenging, but it is perhaps in the interfacing between the controls, the monitoring, and the functional modules that there is a the greatest challenge, for this is where interference signals can influence and corrupt the system. Hardening of a system can be performed in two ways, firstly by the reduction of interference signals by decoupling and shielding techniques, and secondly by the use of logical time sequences and codes. The latter technique is particularly suited to computer control, where the effects of interference can be reduced by duplication, comparison and correlation. It is salutary to remember, however, that no software technique can eliminate interference entering at or after its logic output.

The shielding and decoupling of control systems hardware follows the same techniques as in previous chapter, but an important factor is that most control systems operate at slow speeds, much slower than the majority of interference signals. It is therefore relatively easy to introduce low-pass filters, particularly in semiconductor circuitry, as in the example detailed in the previous section. A series resistor and shunt capacitor in the inputs of

CMOS ICs can make them highly immune to large amplitude transients if the slow speed of response is acceptable.

Fibre-optic links are a primary agent in decoupling control systems, and, as suggested earlier, non-electrical system might be considered in extreme cases, for instance, hydraulic logic. Design, construction and test of complex control systems is likely to be a multidisciplinary process, and though a range of electromagnetic compatibility specifications are available for many components and sub-systems, putting them together may introduce many additional interactions. Here is a further challenge, where careful testing and an understanding of basic processes are vital.

In the 1970s a number of large pulsed-power installations for laser fusion were built in various countries, for instance the LLNL, California SHIVA laser (Gilmartin *et al.*, 1975), and the AWE, Aldermaston HELEN laser (Cooke *et al.*, 1982). Having large numbers of modules, computer control becomes necessary to give flexible operation without requiring large numbers of control staff. Extensive use of fibre optics is also necessary, and considerable attention must be paid to interference problems during design. Though systems may be designed to operate near technical limits, the design of safety systems in pulsed power is a relatively mature technology, and they are designed so that personnel are excluded from high risk areas. That is, expensive equipment may be risked but not personnel. This is relatively easy to achieve in fixed research installations, and in laboratories the core computer can be completely screened, for instance in a shielded room. However, an even greater degree of care and reliability is required to extend these concepts to controlling such systems as automated mass transportation and manufacturing installations, a very challenging field for the future.

REFERENCES

Cooke, R. L., Norman, C. J., & Danson, C. N. (1982) *Proc. SPIE*, **343**, *Laser Diagnostics*, **55**. 1982.

Gilmartin, T. J., Godwin, R. O., Davis, J. W., Hagen, W. F., Horley, C. H., Leppelmeier, G. W., Linford, G. J., Mayale, J. D., O'Neill, W. C., & Trenholm, J. B. (1975) 10 Kilojouls SHIVA laser system for fusion experiments at LLL. *IEEE/OSA Conference on Laser Engineering and Applications, Washington DC, May 1975*.

Index